10 TOP TIPS for **Managing Contact**

Henrietta Bond

BAAF
ADOPTION
& FOSTERING

Published by
**British Association for Adoption & Fostering
(BAAF)**
Saffron House
6–10 Kirby Street
London EC1N 8TS
www.baaf.org.uk

Charity registration 275689

British Library Cataloguing in Publication Data
A catalogue record for this book is available from the British Library

ISBN 978 1 905664 20 7

Project management by Jo Francis, BAAF
Designed by Andrew Haig & Associates
Typeset by Fravashi Aga
Printed in Great Britain by T J International Ltd
Trade distribution by Turnaround Publisher Services, Unit 3,
Olympia Trading Estate, Coburg Road, London N22 6TZ

BAAF is the leading UK-wide membership organisation for all those
concerned with adoption, fostering and child care issues.

Contents

Acknowledgements

Many people have helped with putting together this book. I particularly want to thank Hedi Argent, Elsbeth Neil, David Howe, Sarah Borthwick, and Deborah Cullen, Shaila Shah and Jo Francis at BAAF.

My thanks also to Alison Vincent and Alyson Graham at the Berkshire Information Exchange Service, and A National Voice for allowing me to reproduce information from their organisations.

In addition I also want to thank all those adopted and care-experienced young people who have shared their personal information, their opinions and ideas with me. Their insights are, of course, the most valuable of all in trying to get it right for future generations of young people cared for away from their own families. Thanks also to the excellent adopters and foster carers who have given up their time to be interviewed by me, and the many experienced social workers I have been privileged to meet and work with during the years I have been involved in this field.

Note about the author

Henrietta Bond is a freelance journalist and media consultant specialising in children and family issues. Her interest in looked after children began when she became BAAF's press officer in 1990, and since becoming freelance in 1995 she has worked with Fostering Network, The Who Cares? Trust, NCH, Barnardo's, TalkAdoption, A National Voice and many other children and young people's organisations and local authorities. She has written for *Guardian Society, Community Care, Care and Health, Children Now and Young People Now*. She is the author of *Fostering a Child* and '*If you don't stick with me, who will*?', both published by BAAF.

Henrietta recently trained as a coach and runs her own organisation, Resourceful Coaching Associates. She is currently exploring ways that life coaching can be used to support and develop foster carers and young people preparing to leave care, and staff in the voluntary, public and independent care sectors.

This series

Ten Top Tips for Managing Contact is part of BAAF's Ten Top Tips series. This series tackles fundamental topics in the areas of adoption and fostering with the aim of presenting them in a quick reference format. Each title presents ten good practice tips, each of which is then further elaborated upon.

Future titles will deal with finding families and leaving care.

Introduction

If you are looking for a book which will tell you whether contact is a good or a bad thing, this isn't the right book for you. Equally, if you want something which will offer an "off the peg" model for "doing" contact, this book is also going to disappoint.

However, if you are open to the idea that every child is an individual and every adoptive or permanent foster family and every birth family is unique, then it is far more likely that this book will be useful to you. And if you are committed to approaching contact with the view that, under the right circumstances, with properly identified aims and objectives, contact can be potentially very beneficial to a child, then again, you'll probably find plenty of helpful material within these covers.

A number of studies have set out to examine whether children who are adopted or living in long-term foster placements benefit from contact. Whilst none conclusively show that contact in itself is a beneficial thing, there is sufficient evidence to suggest that contact has the potential to enhance a child's emotional development and their sense of identity. It can also – against common belief – help rather than hinder children in settling into new families, and enable them to make sense of the reasons why they can no longer live with their birth families. Also, most importantly, it can prevent children from trying to live with the painful (and probably impossible) requirement to "forget" their past, by enabling them to keep important people "in mind", even when those people may not be a part of their everyday lives.

What is meant by contact?

In this book, contact is taken to mean anything which involves an exchange of information between the child and their adoptive family, and the child's birth family. "Birth family" can encompass a very wide range of relatives and contact between children and their siblings and grandparents may be as or even more beneficial than contact with birth parents. Former foster carers, children of foster carers and other fostered children living in the foster family, workers who have established a long-term relationship with a child and close friends and neighbours should also be considered as possible parties to include in contact.

Contact encompasses:

- face-to-face meetings;
- telephone calls;
- letter writing;
- exchange of DVDs/videos/tapes;
- emails and texts;
- one side providing information which is not reciprocated, but is stored until such a time when the other party is able or feels ready to access it;
- access to information about the child's heritage, culture and, where relevant, country of origin.

This guide will certainly not argue that contact is right for every child, or that direct contact is better than indirect contact, or vice versa. However, what it will do is argue that *contact should at least be considered in every case*, rather than dismissed out of hand. Life is about a process of change and as children grow, their needs, their perceptions and the information they need about the world around them changes. The young child who may be better protected by not meeting the parent who shunned them and failed to protect them from abuse (and might well be re-traumatised by this experience) may, as a young adult, gain significant benefits from meeting that parent and obtaining answers to pressing questions. So, unless we have processes in place which are sufficiently responsive to the needs of every child as an individual, but also capable of change as the child grows, we may deny children access to information which underpins a fundamental sense of who they are.

While always keeping the child at the focus of any consideration of contact, this book also recognises that contact will only work in the child's best interest if the adult participants fulfil their roles with a commitment to promoting the child's welfare. So the adopter who is properly prepared for issues that may arise, really understands the long-term benefits of contact, is encouraged to air their concerns and has access to support through all stages of the process is more likely to engage positively and resourcefully with the child's birth relatives. By the same token, birth family relatives who have received help to come to terms with the child's new role in their adoptive family and understand the importance of not undermining the child's relationship with their permanent carers will be much better placed to engage positively with the child's permanent family – however much they disagree with the need for the placement.

Another key issue this guide addresses is the role of siblings in children's lives. Too often the importance of contact with their brothers and sisters is overlooked, yet these can be some of the most important and sustaining relationships for an adopted person.

Rather than describing the "right" way to do things, this guide raises many issues that workers need to consider when planning for and supporting this very complex area of human interaction. It offers questions to challenge thinking, checklists of good practice points which need to be considered and examples of different approaches which might be taken.

Henrietta Bond
May 2007

TIP 1

Be clear about the purpose of contact

Imagine what it would be like if you woke up one morning and realised that you would never see any of your family or friends again? Or if you found yourself in a strange bed in a strange house surrounded by people who clearly expected you to love them and become an important part of their lives. Where would your heart and mind be in this situation? How much could you focus on being with these new people while all the time you were wondering what had become of your own family and friends and how you would ever recover from the heartbreak of never seeing them again? It is important to keep this type of scenario in mind when we make decisions about the role of contact in the lives of adopted and permanently fostered children.

Current legislation in the UK favours the concept that children placed in permanent families can benefit from knowledge about, and possibly meetings with, members of their birth family. The notion that children need a "clean break" with their past has been replaced with an awareness that "openness" towards the concept of children being part of two families is beneficial to children's welfare, development and sense of identity.

This is reflected in UK legislation, which states that contact may continue to be beneficial for a child even if they will not be returning to their birth family, as long as the child's welfare is paramount, as such contact can keep alive a sense of the child's origins, and may help to keep open options for family relationships in the child's adult life.

However, this is not an encouragement to assume that every child will benefit from contact in every set of circumstances. Agencies which create a blanket policy which presupposes that all older children will benefit from contact are as likely to get it wrong as are agencies which assume that contact for babies is unnecessary. Ensuring that contact is always kept high on the agenda for consideration does not mean that contact will automatically happen; it simply ensures that all the options have been carefully addressed for each individual child.

Ask yourself who contact is for

Contact is for the child or young person. It may help the birth family to cope with separation and it may enable the adopters to understand more about their child's heritage and previous life, but if the child's needs are not paramount, contact will fail to serve its purpose. Contact should only take place when there are clearly identified benefits for the individual child – never as a sop to ease the pain of the birth family.

When considering how contact may benefit the child, you need to ask the following questions:

- Will contact prevent the child from being torn between dividing loyalties, and enable the child to accept a new family more readily?
- Will contact help the child to settle into their new family by reassuring them that family members are OK and still care about them?
- Will contact help the child to understand why they are unable to live with their birth family?
- Will contact promote the child's development by giving them a

sense of identity and an understanding of how they fit into the world?

- Will contact enable the child to continue relationships that have been positive and beneficial to them in the past?
- Will contact enable the child to develop relationships which will become more important to them as they grow older?
- Will contact help the child to come to terms with past events?
- Will contact re-traumatise a child by bringing them into proximity with someone who abused them or failed to protect them from harm in the past, and make the child question their new family's ability to protect them?
- Will contact reassure a child of their adopters'/long-term foster carers' ability to protect them from harm, while enabling them to salvage positive aspects of former relationships?
- Will contact enable a child to develop an understanding of how people can hold many different types of relationships in their lives, knowing that some people are part of the everyday world and some are seen less frequently and perhaps only on specific occasions?

It is important to remember that these questions can't be answered once and for all. Children's needs change and family circumstances alter over time, and reviews of contact arrangements will be needed as the child grows older.

> *Contact is a minefield of emotion and, in our 12 years' experience, changes and shifts all the time. What you have to remember is that you are not doing it for yourselves or for the birth family, but for your children – for their future, for their needs, and to make their passage to adulthood easier.*
>
> *(Jo, adoptive mother, quoted in 'Contact in Adoption and Permanent Foster Care' (Neil and Howe, 2005))*

How often and with what aim?

When considering issues around how often an individual child should have contact, it is important to be very clear about its aim. If the aim is for a child to maintain or build on a relationship, then the contact must be frequent enough for it to be meaningful for the child. This will be particularly true of younger children for whom a year seems a very long period, during which people can easily be forgotten. So, even if regular visits are not possible, then frequent telephone contact or letters can help to keep the person present in the child's mind.

However, if the purpose of contact is to create a sense of identity for the child, then less frequent meetings or exchanges of information may be more appropriate. It should still not be forgotten that a very young child is likely to need more regular contact than an older child, to "embed" people into their consciousness.

When thinking about the frequency and purpose of any type of contact, you should consider whether the child needs to sustain or develop a relationship, or to develop an awareness of their connections with these people. A card which says 'Happy birthday, with love from your sister, Beth' can mean the world to a child who has regular contact with their sister. For a child who has little or no contact, such an exchange will merely raise questions about how their sibling is (or indeed, who their sibling is!) and how other family members are doing. Without sufficient accompanying information about their sibling, the child may receive few, if any, benefits from this type of exchange.

Will everyone be clear about the purpose of contact and will this affect the way they respond to contact? Does any support need to be offered to help adopters, foster carers or birth families understand this?

Recognise that contact can help children settle into new placements

There used to be a widely held assumption that contact during the early stages of a placement would be very disruptive for the child. Instead, the opposite may be true. A child who has bonded closely to their foster family may experience a powerful feeling of loss which will interfere with their ability to settle in their adoptive family. A child who is torn between their love for and loyalty towards their birth family and their desire to become a member of their new family may become preoccupied with their feelings of separation and their anxieties about what is happening to their birth family. Contact with members of their foster family and birth family can be very important during these early stages, and can reassure the child that these people are still well and present in their lives and continue to care about them.

It is usual to bring the existing foster carers and new adopters together to plan for the child's move into the family; this should include details about the type and frequency of contact the child will have with their previous foster carers. In the early stages it may be important for the child to see the carers fairly regularly, for example, once a week, and also to receive regular phone calls and cards. As the child settles into the new family, the frequency of this contact with the foster family will decrease, although some form of ongoing contact will still be important.

Adopters – who may connect the concept of contact with birth families – may need help to understand why this contact with foster families is so important in helping the child to settle.

Similarly, seeing or speaking to members of the birth family and foster family during the early stages of a new placement can be very reassuring for the child. The child can realise that the birth family has not somehow been obliterated from their lives forever, and that their birth relatives do not think they have vanished or come to serious harm, so does not need to worry about this. Even if the meetings or phone conversations are tinged with pain or sadness, the child can recognise that they are not being expected to shut off all memories of their previous lives and of the people who matter a great deal to them.

Even if more "direct" contact is not possible between the child and birth relatives, it can still be enormously reassuring for the child to know that their birth family is receiving information about them through letters or messages from other relatives.

Foster carers and birth relatives who can clearly show the child that, although they miss them and value them, they wish them well in their

9

permanent family and feel this is a good place for them to be, can play a powerful role in giving "permission" for the child to settle in their new placement.

Don't overlook relationships with other children and young people

Children's relationships with the children of their foster carers and other foster children living with the foster family may also have played a very pivotal role in their lives. A child may have developed a close friendship with another foster child or begun to regard their carer's children as their brothers and sisters. Severing these links can be just as painful as losing contact with birth family members. These important relationships should never be overlooked in making arrangements for contact.

Contact can help children develop a sense of heritage and ethnic identity

Well planned contact has the potential to help all permanently placed children to develop a sense of their identity as they grow up. However, for children who are transracially placed, contact with relatives and/or information about their heritage, culture, religion and customs can be particularly important.

Contact with relatives who live overseas may be potentially difficult to arrange or sustain, but it can be extremely beneficial for children who may otherwise grow up with many questions about their heritage and family circumstances, and the reason they were placed for adoption. The use of email (with appropriate confidentiality built in, where required) can be a good way for children and their adopters to stay in contact with birth families living overseas.

Contact for disabled children

The emotional and identity needs of children and young people with severe learning or communication disabilities may be overlooked if adults assume that contact will confuse or be meaningless for the child. It is probably quite understandable that people might seek to protect a child who they feel is already having to cope with so many difficulties and disadvantages. However, if a child has limited understanding of the situation, it may be extremely difficult for them to make sense of why they are no longer able to see birth relatives and foster carers who have played an important role in their life. Without the ability to ask questions, they may imagine all sorts of terrible things have happened to their birth family and may undergo a major bereavement; this can seriously inhibit their ability to feel secure in their new family.

When should contact not be considered?

Contact should always be considered, but that does not mean it should always happen. There will be times when a positive decision needs to be made that meetings, telephone calls or the exchange of letters may be detrimental to a child's welfare. This might occur if:

- someone is involved who has previously abused, neglected or failed to protect the child, and it is felt probably that contact will re-awaken fears or such painful memories that the child is re-traumatised;
- the child is unable to feel protected by their permanent family and this undermines the child's ability to settle and feel safe;
- the child is so distressed by contact that this significantly outweighs any long-term benefits which may be accrued;
- the child is exposed to a situation where there is a significant risk that they *will* be harmed by someone.

Deciding that contact is not currently appropriate does not mean that the subject of contact becomes a closed book. It is important to do the following:

- Record why it has been decided that particular types of contact are not appropriate and ensure that the relevant parties are aware of this. This information will then be available for the child at a later date if they have questions about the reasons why contact was stopped.
- Build in reviews so that contact can be re-considered as the child grows up and their circumstances change.
- Consider ways in which information can still be exchanged so that the "door is left open" for the growing child to develop a healthy sense of their identity. This might be through opening a letterbox

through an intermediary; the letterbox can lie dormant until all parties feel ready and able to participate. Alternatively, letters and information about the birth family can be kept by the intermediary or by the permanent family until a stage where it is considered that the child feels "safe" enough to see this information.

- Consider whether there is someone else in the birth family who can pass on information. For example, if a child cannot have contact with a sibling who remains in the birth family because this exposes them to too many risks or painful memories, they might be able to receive information from their aunt, for instance, who can reassure them that their sibling is alive and well.

The following case study, taken from Chapter 6 of *See you Soon* (Argent, 1995), explains why contact was ended with a child's father, because it was felt by her mother and other professionals that memories of his formerly abusive behaviour were putting the child at too much risk. It also illustrates the steps the mother took to "keep the door open" for future resumption of her daughter's relationship with her father.

Laura's mother sought help for her daughter after it became apparent that her husband had sexually abused the child. The couple separated but after 16 weeks supervised contact was arranged between Laura (aged four) and her father. Although Laura expressed delight at seeing her father and played games with him, she began bedwetting, having nightmares and biting herself (all signs which had first alerted her mother to the fact that abuse had been taking place).

The change in Laura's behaviour was also noted by her nursery school. There was evidence that the behavioural disturbance seriously impeded her capacity to learn and to manage her peer relationships when she was uncharacteristically involved in an aggressive outburst with another child. It seemed clear that contact with her father was profoundly disturbing for her. The recommendation was that contact should be suspended, until she was of an age to protect herself. Indirect contact in the form of letters and cards was managed and supervised by Laura's mother. She regularly writes the required newsletter, enclosing school photos and pictures that Laura wishes to send. All cards and letters received she keeps to give to her daughter when she is older. No requests have been made by Laura to see her father. She understands that he is not seeing her because he hurt her. There are no behavioural disturbances and she is doing well in school and other aspects of her development.

This case is a reminder that, although children may still love relatives who have harmed them, they may be unable to cope with the impact of having contact with them while they are young and vulnerable. They may express their feelings through behaviour rather than words.

TIP 2

Agree what's going to work best for the needs of the individual child

> *I only see her when I feel comfortable about seeing her. She's nice. She's got problems...But I do see her...*
>
> *(An adopted girl whose mother is cared for in a nursing home, quoted in 'Adopted Children Speaking' (Thomas and Beckford with Lowe and Murch, 1999))*

In order to work out the role of contact in the life of a child, it is essential that every child is seen as an individual. This seems an obvious point to make, but sometimes agencies have a tendency to develop a model of contact and try to fit children and their families into this. By starting each time with the needs of the individual child and the circumstances which surround them, you can then identify the purpose of contact (as discussed in the previous chapter) and use this as a starting point to carry out an assessment. Consider the following.

- How can contact serve this child's needs in the long term as well as the short term?
- What sort of contact is likely to be most beneficial to this child, for example, face-to-face or letter box?
- What sort of contact is likely to work best for the circumstances of the adults involved (given that arrangements are more likely to succeed if the adults co-operate in the child's interests)?
- What will the child lose if certain types of contact are ruled out, for example, face-to-face meetings with siblings?
- Do the positives outweigh the negatives in situations where the child may come into contact with birth relatives who have abused them or failed to protect them from harm?

Him and his mum had the same conversation every time, they talked about the past, about times when things had been good in the family...after contact he was relaxed. He had satisfied himself that they were still there and he could get on with his life.

(Quoted in 'Contact in Adoption and Permanent Foster Care' (Neil and Howe, 2005))

Be clear what different types of contact mean

In considering the above, it's important to be clear about the different types of contact so you can ensure that you know exactly what is being discussed. You should also ensure that the adopters or long-term foster carers and birth relatives, and any other workers or guardians, have the same understanding of what they are discussing or agreeing to.

● Direct contact is the term frequently applied to face-to-face meetings and telephone conversations.

● Indirect contact is often the term used to describe contact via an intermediary, for example, letterbox contact where an agency passes on letters so that the address of the adopters/permanent foster carers remains confidential.

However, don't assume that all letter-writing will be "indirect" contact. If the adopters or long-term foster carers agree to pass on their address to the birth family so the birth family can send letters and cards, this could be considered "direct" contact. Similarly, a child may be able to make or receive calls to their birth family via a mobile with a restricted number. Is this direct or indirect contact? And what about contact via email or video/DVD? Is an email – where details remain anonymous – any different to a letter passed on through an intermediary? Being addressed directly by a child on video/DVD can feel like a very "direct" experience for the birth relative, even if they have no idea where that child currently lives.

Be specific

Instead of using terms like "indirect" or "direct" contact, it is better to be specific about what is meant. For example, having a written agreement for phone calls three times a year, or an exchange of letters twice a year through the local authority letterbox scheme and cards on festive occasions and birthdays leaves little room for misunderstanding. Even better is to spell out who will make the first step, for example, will the adopters and child write and the birth family write back? Will the teenage child be the one to call when they want to see their birth family?

Ask the child what they want

Too often everyone puts a great deal of effort into planning for the best interests of the child, but still manages to overlook the child's wishes and feelings. Even young people who are normally articulate about their needs may not recognise that they are entitled to a "say" in these matters. They may also find it difficult to speak out about their feelings because of divided loyalties, or may simply go along with the arrangements made by the adults, believing that these are immutable and inflexible.

It is important to ensure that children feel empowered to speak out about their wishes and feelings about contact. Even if you have kept the child or young person fully informed and involved in events leading up to their permanent placement, they may still have so many different issues to think about that they do not fully register the impact of one set of arrangements ending and another coming into place. It is a good idea to make time to talk to the child on their own about contact issues, without anyone else present. By clearly focusing on the child's views, the child is free to say who they want or do not want to see, and how often they would like contact to take place. Obviously you may need to explain to the child or young person that some aspects of their wishes may not be able to be fulfilled, and why this is the case – for example, the frequency of contact may be impractical – but at least the child's fundamental views have been heard and recorded. You then need to ensure that these are kept to the fore when contact agreements are discussed.

> *But if he's changed and be nice, be really good and sensible then I would be able to contact...But if he's not, then I wouldn't. Because after his behaviour, of what he did to me, I don't think I would...*
>
> *(Karen (13) explaining that she did not want contact with her father unless he had changed his behaviour, quoted in 'Adopted Children Speaking' (Thomas and Beckford with Lowe and Murch, 1999))*

Don't overlook foster carers

If a child has lived with foster carers prior to adoption, the importance of this relationship must not be overlooked. For some children who have lived with carers since birth, these carers may be their emotional "parents". As highlighted in the previous chapter, foster carers can play an important role in helping children to settle into their new family.

It is usually best if this contact with former foster carers takes place in the adopters' home. Returning to their previous home can be very unsettling for children who may immediately revert back to a sense of a familiar environment and find it distressing and unsettling to be expected to leave after a relatively short visit. Having the foster carer visit the child in their new home or, if this is not possible for geographical reasons, meeting up somewhere neutral in between, is a better way of reinforcing the child's status in their new family.

Recognise the role of siblings

It is widely recognised that contact with siblings can be one of the most beneficial forms of contact. It is also important to recognise that children may regard their foster carer's children or other children fostered or adopted by their carers as "siblings", and gain significant benefits from these relationships.

For some children, their relationship with an older sibling who has acted as their main carer may be the most important relationship in their life. However, there may also be situations where siblings have mistreated one another, where one child has been highly favoured over the other or siblings have been involved in sexual activities together. It is essential to try to gather as much information as possible about the nature of different relationships in a sibling group in order to ensure that children get the best from contact and are not re-exposed to distressing or threatening situations.

A child placed for adoption or placed in permanent foster care is likely to worry about what is happening to their siblings. They may worry about whether their brothers and sisters are happy in their new families. Providing early opportunities for children to meet their siblings with their adoptive families – even if regular face-to-face contact is not possible – may provide reassurance that siblings are being cared for. This will help to allow the child to focus more on their own situation and their own needs.

How to help permanently placed children who worry about the sibling who they believe is not being cared for properly in the birth family remains a dilemma. In some cases, adopters have discontinued contact because they felt a young child was taking on too many concerns about siblings in the birth family. There are also cases of older children who have walked out of adoptive placements because they felt an overwhelming responsibility to return home to look after siblings. The best approach is to be prepared to offer as much support as possible to the child and to the adopters or permanent carers faced with these difficult situations.

Don't assume babies don't need face-to-face contact

It has frequently been assumed that face-to-face contact is only for older children who already know their families, and that babies and very young children don't need contact because they don't remember their birth families. However, there is a body of research which suggests that, by focusing on contact only for older children, we are overlooking opportunities to promote the welfare and sense of identity of children placed as infants.

In Chapter 1 of *Staying Connected,* edited by Hedi Argent, (2002, p10) managing face-to-face contact for young adopted children is discussed.
Research reinforces what we know from experience: that the younger the child at placement the more adaptable he or she is to the adoptive situation in particular but also to the whole range of wider experiences. Essentially, the better adjusted to the adoptive situation the child is, the more it should be expected that he or she will have the psychological resources to cope with, and make positive use of, post-adoption contact arrangements.

Argent argues that there is an irony around the fact that face-to-face contact is most frequently planned for children placed at an older age – where it is likely that there will be far more complex emotional issues to navigate – yet is infrequently planned for younger children. She believes that the lack of attachment to the birth relatives by the child can make it a less emotionally charged experience for everyone involved.

The arguments against considering contact for children placed as infants normally centre around the fact that the child won't miss what they don't know. However, as adopted children grow older, their awareness of the "gaps" in their history and personal sense of identity are likely to develop. For some children, this can become an all-consuming, urgent quest to pursue vital personal knowledge which they feel is being withheld from them. Allowing the child to grow up with this information already available to them can prevent the fact of their adoption becoming an issue which overshadows other aspects of their development and wellbeing.

In considering contact for infants, you need to do the following.

● Ensure that adopters of infants have access to plenty of information which helps them to understand that adopted children may grow up with a pressing need to know about their history and identity. This could include material from research studies but should also include opportunities to hear from adopted people and adopters who have negotiated this type of contact successfully.

● Help adopters understand that the relationship their young adopted child will develop with their birth relatives is unlikely to pose any threat to their own roles in the child's life. Research suggests that the child placed as an infant is more likely to consider a birth relative simply as a more distant aunt or uncle, or a family friend, rather than a close relative.

● Help adopters recognise the benefits of meeting with the birth family even if no face-to-face contact is planned between the child and their birth family. This meeting can provide information which will be very useful for future indirect communication with the birth family and for answering children's questions about their birth family. Some adopters may feel more positive about considering face-to-face contact in the future if they have previously met the birth family.

● Help adopters to recognise that building a relationship with birth relatives now may prevent a lot of emotional stress in the future. With knowledge about their birth parents, the growing child won't create fantasies around these mysterious people they have never met.

● Help adopters to think about the additional benefits their young child may gain from having contact with their birth family, for example, an "only" adopted child may have the benefit of siblings in their birth family.

● Help adopters to consider the important role birth grandparents can play. They can often provide information and a sense of continuity, and may be better able to engage with the adoptive family than birth parents, who can find the process too painful. For adoptive families where there are no living grandparents, an adopted child's grandparent may be viewed as a very welcome addition to the family.

● Help adopters to recognise that a year is a very long time in the life of a young child. A young child is unlikely to remember or feel comfortable with someone they only see once a year. In the early years contact may need to be more frequent in order to establish a sense of relationship.

Whatever is decided, be clear that the interests of the growing child must be paramount.

I kept asking ... Mum and Dad what the court said. And you know when you're 18 you can move house, but when I'm 18 of course I can go and see my real mum...Yes, yes, I definitely do tell my mum about fifty times that I want to go and see my real mum. And they said they would sort it out.

(Rhianna (aged 12) who is very keen to meet her birth mother when she is older, quoted in 'Adopted Children Speaking' (Thomas and Beckford with Lowe and Murch, 1999))

TIP 3

Put systems in place to facilitate contact

I try and write once every month, but now I'm writing more often, because in her last letter she said she would like to hear from me more. So I said, 'Yes'.

(Anna (aged 14) who communicates with her birth mother through social services, quoted in 'Adopted Children Speaking' (Thomas and Beckford with Lowe and Murch, 1999))

Good contact does not just happen. It needs careful planning and systems in place to support and sustain it. This chapter examines some of the practical aspects of putting together the framework for beneficial contact. These range from planning the contact, creating collaboration and putting together an agreement to the practical aspects of managing and supporting contact, such as administering a letterbox system.

Preparation for contact starts during recruitment

Preparation for contact begins long before a child is placed with a new family. Unless training and preparation for adopters and foster carers includes information which truly helps prospective families to understand the benefits for children, the likelihood of them valuing and supporting contact when a child is placed is slim. Be as creative as possible through all the stages of preparation and enable prospective families to hear from adopters and foster carers who have successfully managed contact about the different approaches which worked for them. Hearing the viewpoint of adopted adults and young people who have had positive experiences of contact, or experienced the trauma of separation without contact, can also be powerful tools in developing positive attitudes among prospective adopters.

June Thoburn, writing in *Contact in Adoption and Permanent Foster Care*, (Neil and Howe, 2004) highlights some of the characteristics she has identified through studies and interviews with adopters which she feels enable prospective adopters to work towards establishing and maintaining successful contact arrangements.

I would pull out particularly "enjoying a challenge" (a term that appeared frequently when motivations were discussed); a blend of altruism and self-directed motives, with the insight to understand what they hope to get back from the child as well as what they can give; and above all the capacity to empathise with the birth parents as a way into an understanding of the child's history and coping strategies. They took any challenges raised by contact in their stride, as they took in their stride the much more major challenges of parenting a confused and troubled child.

Planning comes first!

Contact needs to be carefully planned. An assessment of need and any agreements arising from this should be finalised before the practical arrangements for contact are discussed. If you find yourself focusing on where the face-to-face meetings between the child, their adoptive family and their siblings and grandparents are going to take place *before* you've agreed the purpose of contact, you probably need to take a step back.

Who decides?

In some cases, court orders decide how and how often contact should take place, but it is widely recognised that contact which can be negotiated between permanent families and birth families has the most chance of success. Before opting to pursue a court order consider:

- Is a court order absolutely necessary or is there room for negotiation?
- Whose interests is the court order serving?
- Does a court order guarantee that everyone will collaborate?
- Are you likely to alienate permanent families and discourage them from realising the benefits of contact, if contact is imposed on them?
- Will people simply agree to the arrangement because the court says they must do so, but then look for the first loophole in order to get out of it?

Seek collaboration

Contact works best when it happens through collaboration. When permanent families and birth families come together, putting aside their personal feelings and misgivings, and unite in order to do what is best for the child, contact has the potential to be a very positive experience. It is human nature to react against something which is imposed upon us. So the adopter who is already anxious about contact is much more likely to dwell on the difficulties of an imposed requirement for twice-yearly meetings with their child's mother – who they've already been told can be "difficult". However, if they have met that mother, recognised the complex and unhappy circumstances of her life, and can then sit down with her and a social worker to put an agreement together, there is a much better chance of the adopter taking a sense of "ownership" in these arrangements.

> *We were emotionally blackmailed into it. I feel very resentful because of the way they did it. We have seen them three times now and it's a real blight on my life. In fact it's ruined my life.*
>
> (An adoptive parent explaining that she agreed to the birth parents' request for contact only because she and her partner feared that the child would be removed if they did not comply, quoted in 'Contact in Adoption and Permanent Foster Care' (Neil and Howe, 2004))

Ask yourself how you can help your adopters or permanent foster carers to be prepared and open to work collaboratively with birth families.

- Do your preparation groups offer sufficient opportunities for adopters and foster carers to fully grasp the significance of contact and to think about this in the context of their own lives?
- Do prospective adopters and foster carers have access to adoptive families who have managed contact, or have opportunities to hear from birth families and adopted adults?
- Do prospective permanent families have opportunities to express their concerns and think through issues that may arise? Or are they reluctant to voice these feelings in case this jeopardises their chance of a placement?
- Do new permanent families know that there is support to hand to help them work through difficulties or concerns?
- Do permanent families recognise that contact isn't "set in stone", but is a flexible process which should be regularly reviewed and adapted as the child grows?
- Do permanent families have an opportunity to meet birth families before contact arrangements begin?

How to put together an agreement

However different their situations and backgrounds, permanent families and birth families have one major thing in common – the child. By keeping the child's welfare firmly at the centre of the process, it is possible to unite all the adults in a sense of co-operation. The role of the worker is therefore to find ways to bring these different parties together and help them maintain their focus on the child's needs.

Sometimes it will be best to conduct initial negotiations by discussing these with the individual parties and then bringing permanent families and birth families together to sign the agreement. In some cases, permanent and birth families may be willing and able to sit down together at an earlier stage and work through all the stages of the planning together. However, in other cases negotiations may take place separately and families may not meet when they sign the agreement. Workers will need to be sensitive and responsive to what will work best in each case, bearing in mind the circumstances of families and the paramount needs of the child.

When putting together agreements with permanent families and birth family members, aim to:

- keep the child's needs central to the process;
- allow scope for flexibility;
- aim for clarity and be specific about the different types of contact involved;
- spell things out in down-to-earth, practical language;
- focus on how to build the quality of the relationships;
- err on the side of quality rather than quantity;
- spell out the role of the agency and the support arrangements;
- build in a review mechanism – ideally with a clear timescale.

An example of a contact agreement can be found in Appendix 1.

Support

The issue of effective support is dealt with in greater detail under Tip 7, but the availability of social work support should be an integral part of any plans and agreements around contact.

Letterbox systems

There are mixed opinions about the best way to manage contact by letter. Some agencies have carefully devised systems which support all parties but also operate some form of control over issues such as confidentiality and the appropriateness of letter content. Some operate letterbox systems but never open letters or intervene unless they are made aware of problems. Other agencies believe that contact arrangements are best left to the participating parties. All these approaches have their own merits.

Some key factors to bear in mind when deciding on the details of letterbox contact include:

- What will be the benefits or disadvantages of opening letters before passing them on?
- What support can be provided if inappropriate material is being communicated?
- How can you help to ensure that letters are passed on in good time, so that children are not disappointed and adults dispirited?

An outline model of one particular letterbox system is given in Appendix 2. Tip 7 also looks at how workers can help adopters and birth families prepare for and manage aspects of indirect contact, such as producing guidelines for letter writing and assistance for families where English is not their first language.

Managing modern technology

As technology evolves, it provides increased and diverse ways for people to communicate. Whilst this may be beneficial for many, it creates significant challenges for managing contact. Children and young people tend to carry their mobiles around with them and if they exchange numbers with birth relatives it can be almost impossible for permanent families to regulate the amount of contact, or to gate-keep what is being discussed. The same applies to email where, again, contact cannot be so easily monitored by permanent families. A situation may occur where a child who is communicating directly with their birth relatives could find themselves coping alone with a raft of difficult emotions. Sadly, there have been some cases of placements disrupting when birth families have obtained a child's phone or email details and have used these to undermine the child's developing relationship with their new family.

There are no easy answers to the problem of how to manage the effects of technology, so it is important to encourage permanent families to be aware of the issues which may arise and to think creatively about how to respond to them. Most importantly, they need to look out for changes in the child's moods or behaviour and to be aware that contact (whether openly taking place, or happening without their knowledge) may be raising issues which the child needs help to deal with.

> *My mum...She can't cope, so if she's fell over and cut herself, she'd be crying down the phone. I wish that could be different. And she's pretty low on the phone. It's like she's worried.*
>
> *(A boy who spoke about some painful aspects of phone contact with his mother, but did not say he wanted it to stop, quoted in 'Adopted Children Speaking' (Thomas and Beckford with Lowe and Murch, 1999))*

Below are some points to bear in mind when considering this issue.

- Find out as much as you can about technology to pick up useful hints and tips to pass on to adopters and foster carers. Perhaps a work colleague has a lot of knowledge about this and can start to compile a list of tips? What advice can your IT support provide? Listen to children and young people, who often know more about these things than anyone else and may also be able to tell you about methods of getting around obstacles adults try to put in place! The more knowledge you can accumulate, the more you can support permanent families with these issues.
- Ensure that permanent families and birth families understand why the passing on of mobile numbers and email addresses may create difficulties for the child.
- Discourage people from bringing mobiles to face-to-face contact meetings because numbers can be exchanged using infra-red technology simply by pointing phones at each other.
- If a situation arises where a birth relative is about to pass on their contact information or ask the child for theirs, it is useful for the worker or adopter to have a stock phrase ready, for example: 'This isn't part of our arrangement for today, we can talk about

this later. Let's just concentrate on enjoying the day.'

- Encourage permanent families to be honest with children about why they must be careful about giving out their mobile phone number or email address. It can be hard for children who swap numbers freely with casual friends to comprehend why they cannot also do this with their siblings who live within the birth family.

- Consider appropriate ways for a child's mobile number to be changed after they come into placement, for example, buying the child a new phone. (But remember that even young children can be very knowledgeable about technology and may be fully aware that phone numbers can be transferred across services.) If a child is seriously at risk from phone calls you may need to seek help about how a phone number can be discontinued.

- Don't overlook texting! Just because the child is never heard chatting on the phone does not mean they are not receiving messages which may affect them.

- Don't forget all the other ways children and young people communicate, for example, internet networking sites like MySpace and Bebo enable young people to create their own profiles and to stay in touch with friends.

- Help permanent families to think of ways they can discuss mobile, text and internet use openly with children so that they do not find themselves "policing" these or taking action surreptitiously. This can easily undermine trust within the family.

- Encourage permanent families to consider providing a mobile phone exclusively for contact with the birth family. The phone can be kept by the adopters and switched off for most of the time, so if the number is passed on to other birth family members there is little risk of the child being bombarded with calls from birth relatives. The child can also ask for the phone when they want to contact the birth family, so the impetus for contact remains with the child.

- If your agency or service monitors letterbox contact, workers will need to be alert to the passing on of phone and email details through letters.

- If email is being sent via the letterbox service for workers to pass on, ask for the correspondence to be enclosed as an attachment.

In this way the attachment can be forwarded directly from the agency, with only the agency's email address appearing.

● Recognise that email, text and phone contact can be a very positive way for separated siblings to stay in regular contact, especially if these siblings are living with different adopters or foster carers where there is less risk of the number being acquired by adult birth relatives.

Recognise that it may be impossible to regulate the way mobiles and the internet are used by older children – and older children may already have their birth family phone numbers (whether landlines or mobiles) indelibly engraved on their memories. Therefore, permanent families need to create an environment where young people are able to openly discuss their feelings about their birth families.

TIP 4

Keep memories and histories alive

> *It's about knowing what makes Dave tick. We didn't find that out from the paperwork but we can get what makes him tick from his mother – not from information but from the feel of the whole family. Because Dave is so complicated you have to get to know as much as you can to get inside his head.*
>
> *(Adoptive mother in a situation where there is direct contact with birth mother, siblings, maternal grandmother and aunt, quoted in 'Adoption and Permanent Placement' (Neil and Howe, 2005))*

Children can hold two families in their hearts and minds without suffering conflicts of loyalty – if the situation is managed carefully. After all, most of us have two sets of grandparents, and possibly several aunts and uncles, cousins, nieces and nephews. We may have a very strong attachment to a particular cousin we only see at major family occasions, or hold very fond memories of an uncle who emigrated to Australia when we were young. We accept, quite naturally, that there are a finite number of people in our everyday lives, and a whole world of other people who are important to us, but only encountered at certain times.

However, if we knew we would *never* see or hear from our favourite cousin or our Australian uncle again, we would probably begin a process of mourning; which is what happens to children who believe they will never encounter their birth relatives again. If you help adopters and permanent foster carers to think about their own families in relation to this dynamic, they will find it easier to understand why contact can be very important to their child.

Encourage permanent families to encompass birth families

We need to encourage adopters and permanent foster carers to create a sense of family which *encompasses* the child's birth family. In this way, the child is able to hold onto positive relationships from other areas of their life without fearing a conflict with their role in their new family.

"Encompassing" the birth family doesn't mean that adopters and permanent carers will necessarily be expected to receive birth relatives into their home (although some may choose to do this), nor does it actually have to involve any form of communication between the families. There are cases where children – for reasons of safety and emotional security – cannot communicate with their birth relatives, but the permanent family can help the child to "hold them in mind" by talking about them and acknowledging their role in the child's life.

Michael's mother had died six months previously and, bereaved, he would cry for her. It broke my heart to see him so unhappy and I felt helpless. I would try to explain to him that his mother had loved him very much, that she had not wanted to die but sometimes people got sick and couldn't help it. I told him she would never have wanted to leave him but I was his second mummy and I would love him just as much...It took many months before Michael settled, and now he says he is lucky to have two mums, both of whom love him so much. We often look at photographs of his mother and on special occasions we have sent helium balloons, with messages attached to them, into the sky. Last year we planted a rose for her on Mother's Day and it was so heavy with flowers this summer that I felt she must have been watching over him.

(Permanent foster carer, quoted in 'If you don't stick with me, who will?' (Bond, 2005))

Create awareness and understanding

In order for contact to work effectively, children and young people need to develop a "bedrock" of understanding about their situation. Unless careful work is done to help the child come to terms with the fact that they will not be returning to their birth family – and wherever possible, the reasons for this – contact can be a baffling and distressing experience.

It is important to explore the child's understanding of events and to help them make sense out of the reality; otherwise they can create fantasies about what "really" happened. A child who has no opportunity to do this may end up blaming themselves or blaming siblings for them not being able to stay with their birth family. They may see their removal as some kind of punishment or question the accuracy of their memories about events which took place. There are a number of ways in which workers can provide support to the child, but also to permanent families and birth relatives to help them support the child in gaining this understanding.

- Engage in direct work with the child, and therapeutic interventions if needed.
- Ensure that materials such as life story books contain explanations which do not distort or gloss over the reasons why the child was removed from their birth family.
- Help permanent families to understand the importance of life story work and why memories need to be revisited.
- Ensure that the child or young person has ongoing opportunities to talk about their questions, memories, anxieties and hopes surrounding their birth family.
- Enlist the support of birth relatives who can help the child create a better understanding of the reason why they could not remain with their birth family.
- Encourage birth relatives to give explanations as to why the child had to leave, in letters, which can be kept and opened later in life when the content will be more meaningful to the child.

When children are adopted as infants

For young children, especially those who have no real memories of their birth families, being adopted is unlikely to be a significant issue. At a young age these children will probably take it in their stride, much more than adults, for whom contact raises a whole range of concerns and uncertainties.

Young adopted children with no memory of their birth relatives will need slow and careful preparation for contact. Contact needs to be seen as part of an ongoing process which enables the child to develop a sense of their identity. Contact which is not embedded in the adoptive family's "openness" towards the child's link with their birth family is likely to confuse rather than benefit the child.

From an early stage, adopters need to introduce the concept of being part of another family to the child's life, so that the word "adoption" and the concept it embodies form a natural part of the child's world. If the information that they are adopted is sprung upon the child as a precursor to contact, the child may be left trying to make sense of their place in the adoptive family at the same time as when they are trying cope with the impact of contact with "relative strangers" from their birth family.

I don't feel that it bothered Damien in the slightest...you know he didn't dwell on it, he just accepted it...I think it was very healthy that he'd seen her and got a memory at five or six...you know, he has that memory whereas at three he didn't have it and he would never have had it...I mean if you asked him to describe [his birth mum] I'm sure he could now, whereas he couldn't before.

(Adoptive mother speaking, quoted in 'Contact in Adoption and Permanent Foster Care' (Neil and Howe, 2004))

Support from other children and adopted adults

Adopted and permanently fostered children may experience a whole range of conflicting emotions, for example, they may find it hard to balance their loyalty to their birth family with their loyalty to their adoptive family. These feelings may be very difficult for them to voice, because they fear hurting members of the adoptive family if they talk about this. Children and young people in this situation may feel very isolated and believe that they are the "only ones" going through these experiences. They may benefit a great deal from opportunities to meet other adopted and permanently fostered young people and adopted adults.

Some resourceful permanent families may recognise the benefits for their child in meeting other children and young people in similar situations, but may not know how to go about arranging this. Workers from the agency will be best placed to offer opportunities for young people to come together to discuss their experiences of being adopted or permanently fostered.

Don't overlook other children in the adoptive family

When focusing on the needs of the individual child in contact arrangements it is important not to forget that other children may also be affected. What support will adopters or foster carers offer to children living in their family who do not have contact with their birth relatives to help them cope and make sense of their situation? Will these children be involved in contact with their adopted siblings' birth relatives? Will the birth children of the adoptive family or other adopted siblings feel that their relationship with the child is diminished if the child begins to have regular contact with their birth family? How will these other children living in the adoptive family be supported to recognise that their own position as "brothers" and "sisters" is not diminished or replaced by the child having contact with their birth family?

TIP 5

Prepare children individually for contact

Social workers should be able to recognise and accept that the needs of the young person may differ from the needs of their parents.

(Zena Dickson, who was previously in care, quoted in 'See you Soon' (Argent, 1995))

Each child approaches contact with a different history, different experiences, different memories, fears and aspirations. What helps one child prepare for exchanging information or face-to-face meetings with birth relatives may cause another child to have recurring nightmares. What works well for one child in the family may not work well for their brothers and sisters. This chapter looks at some of the practical aspects of preparing children for contact, and highlights some of the key issues which need to be addressed and questions which should be asked about what will be best for the individual child.

When the child moves from foster care

When a child is moving into a permanent placement after short-term foster care placements, they will need help to adapt to the change in circumstances and how this affects contact. During the temporary foster placement, the aim of contact would have been to return the child to their birth family, so contact arrangements would have been more frequent and focused on strengthening the connection between the child and their birth family. To help the child settle into and recognise their role in their permanent family, it is important that contact arrangements change to reflect this situation. If arrangements continue as before, the child may become confused and birth relatives may try to ignore the reality of what has happened. Clearly this does not mean that all contact with birth relatives should be ended, but there should be a sense of transition which is reflected in the nature and frequency of contact. Everyone needs a clear understanding of how the situation is changing and how contact will reflect this. The child will need this clearly explained to them and reinforced by their permanent family.

It can be helpful to encourage birth relatives to use contact prior to the adoption to share positive memories with the child, express their sadness about what has gone wrong and tell the child they hope that they will settle well into their permanent family. You will need to prepare and support birth relatives to do this and to understand the valuable role they can play in ensuring that the child has the best chance of settling and flourishing in their permanent family.

Children with disabilities

The more difficult it is for a child or young person to grasp a situation or communicate their feelings about it, the more need there is to ensure that support is available to help the child make sense of what is happening. It is also very important for permanent families and workers with children with severe disabilities to recognise that a child's behaviour may be the only way they can express their feelings.

> *He missed his birth relatives and wanted to see them. That was clear despite his disability. He was asking for them all the time in the only way he could. He was crying every day. 'Car-go-see nanny.' He remembers people's cars. We had a car so he could not understand why we could not take him to see his granny. He cried for over a year. He went through a real bereavement.*
>
> *(Adoptive parent, quoted in 'Staying Connected' (Argent, 2002))*

A child with learning disabilities may not be able to remember people over a long period of time. Infrequent contact may be bewildering for them and more regular contact may be needed to help them to get the maximum benefit from meetings. However, too much contact or face-to-face contact which lasts for too long a period may be overwhelming for the child, so a balance needs to be established to meet the needs of the individual. What services can your agency provide to ensure that adopters and foster carers are trained and supported to communicate most effectively with disabled children about their wishes, feelings and concerns?

How will the child participate in "indirect" contact?

It can be tempting for permanent families and birth families to become so involved in their different roles and responsibilities around contact arrangements that sometimes the child's role in this process can be overlooked. Tip 7 looks at how agencies can support the adult participants, but this chapter looks specifically at how children can be encouraged to participate in indirect contact.

There are a number of ways in which even very young or severely disabled children can participate in indirect contact arrangements:

- by creating paintings and drawings, or selecting from their existing painting and drawings;
- by helping to choose photographs to be included with letters;

- by helping to choose and sign cards for birth relatives (even if this is just making a mark or adding a kiss);
- by suggesting news and information which can be passed on to the birth family;
- by creating a recording on tape, CD or video of nursery rhymes, songs or poems.

As children get older they may want to play a greater – or lesser – part in indirect contact. Some children may decide to do their own letter writing and may send letters in addition to or instead of letters sent by their adoptive parents. Some may want to pull out of the arrangement altogether and may object to their permanent family forwarding information about them to their birth family. Adopters and permanent foster carers may need support to help a young person understand why contact is being maintained. Young people may need opportunities to talk through their feelings with an independent support worker or to discuss them with other adopted young people.

How will adopters and agency staff react if a young person clearly states that they do not want any further information sent to their birth family? How do you balance the young person's wishes against the knowledge that they will probably want more information about their birth family at a later stage in their lives and may regret closing off this source of information? How will a young person feel if they find that their adoptive family have been communicating with their birth family either without telling them or in direct opposition to their wishes? Are there ways in which the agency can "keep the door open" on behalf of both families, without damaging the young person's trust in their adoptive family?

Will the child receive cards and letters on special occasions?

Some seemingly straightforward matters, such as whether a child will receive cards and presents, can become very significant when there is insufficient clarity and the child does not know what to expect.

Some agencies advise against having contact around birthdays and major occasions such as Christmas. Others feel that children may feel "forgotten" if they no longer receive cards from birth family members. It is best to have these matters clarified in the initial agreement for contact.

Try to focus on the needs of the individual child rather than simply following a blanket policy about these matters. If arrangements are imposed on participants simply because your agency "always does it that way", permanent families and birth families are less likely to abide by them. When making these decisions you need to consider the following points.

- Will this child feel let down if they don't receive a card at this important time?
- Will contact at this time introduce too much additional pressure at an already emotionally-charged moment?
- How reliable are the birth family likely to be around sending cards on time?
- If the exchange is through a letterbox system, how can you ensure that cards will be forwarded in time?
- If cards are sent, will there also be a letter included? Would it be better to have a letter sent separately at another, less emotionally-charged time?
- In the case of a child placed as an infant, how natural is it for them to receive a birthday card from someone they see only occasionally and with whom they may only have a fairly superficial relationship?
- Alternatively, does receiving a card offer an opportunity for the child to develop a gradual awareness of birth family relatives?

Whatever is decided, it is important to be very clear about this decision and explain the reasons to all parties involved. It is best to have this information in writing, probably as part of the contact agreement.

Will presents be given to the child?

Again, some agencies advise against presents whilst others feel they are appropriate if ground rules have been agreed. If possible, try to focus on the needs of the individual child, rather than following a blanket policy. It is helpful to address the following issues.

- What role are presents playing here?
- Will birth relatives feel obliged to buy very expensive presents as a way of assuring the child that they still care?
- Is there a need to set a price limit and sense of equality? For example, if the adopted child is exchanging gifts with several

siblings living with a foster carer, what will be affordable from the foster carer's side?

● Is there a risk that the child will see the birth family simply as a source of expensive gifts?

● When someone only sees a child occasionally or has very limited contact with them, how will they ensure that the present is relevant to the child's age and interests? (Some agencies recommend that only gift tokens are given, to avoid this problem.)

● Will an older child feel forgotten if, for example, their birth grandparents suddenly stop sending gifts?

How will the child be prepared for direct contact?

Some children will need a considerable period of time to prepare for a face-to-face visit and to work through their emotions before the visit takes place. Other children may fret or become overwrought if they are told too early, so it is better if they are prepared closer to the event. In each case, the personality and situation of the individual child must be the deciding factor – as well as the opinions of the permanent family, who know the child better than anyone else.

Children with learning disabilities may have little concept of time so it may not be appropriate to tell them about a contact visit in advance. The child's adopters or permanent carers are probably the best people to decide when is the best time to tell the child.

> *She's a timeless creature so you can't prepare her in advance.*
>
> *(Adoptive mother of a girl with Down's syndrome, quoted in 'Staying Connected' (Argent, 2002))*

In the following chapter we look at some of the issues which may arise and how to help the child prepare for and cope with these.

TIP 6

Support children to manage expectations

> *That's been the hardest thing, him saying he wants to see her and what do you keep saying?...[your birth mother] doesn't want to see you, obviously you can't say it like that...I just say at the moment it is too upsetting for her.*
>
> *(Adoptive parent speaking, quoted in 'Contact in Adoption and Permanent Foster Care' (Neil and Howe, 2005))*

Contact with birth relatives is unlikely to be easy. By the very nature of the situation, it is bound to raise painful memories or renew the child's sense of loss. Problems can also arise from the involved adults' desire to protect children from painful realities which are then brought into stark focus when a child actually meets birth family members, or if something occurs which reminds them of the problems which led to their removal from their birth family. Children and young people may need a lot of help to manage their fantasies about their birth family and to cope with disappointments when reality fails to match up with their expectations.

In relation to all aspects of contact, it is generally better to help children manage the pain they experience, rather than try to cover it over.

Keep information real

There can be a tendency to present children with an over-sanitised version of the reasons why they are no longer able to live with their birth families. Whilst the reasons behind this are usually very well intended, presenting too rosy a picture of the birth family can have negative effects.

- Children may find it hard to understand why they cannot live with their birth family, and this can create uncertainties about their role in their permanent family.
- Children may develop unrealistic expectations of their birth family and be left feeling let down when they don't fulfil these expectations.
- Children may have memories of abuse or neglect in their birth family and attempts to gloss over these by adopters may lead the child to question their own memory and understanding of events.

It is better to offer children a more realistic picture, allowing for their age and level of understanding, whilst at the same time helping them to accept something of the reasons why their birth family may have behaved in a particular way. The child who still loves the parent who neglected or mistreated them may not find it especially difficult to understand that the parent who did this still loves them, despite their actions. They may be far more able to cope with the concept of someone having different facets to their personality than may adopters who have never directly experienced this dichotomy of personality.

If a child grows up with too sanitised or rosy a picture of their birth relatives and then meets them as they get older, they may find it hard to adjust to the reality. Some adopters have said that they felt quite guilty when their children eventually met their birth family and discovered that the family situation and the reasons for the child not being able to live at home were not as the adopters had described.

Adopters may need help and support to think through the most appropriate way to explain information about the birth family to the child in ways which are not judgemental or derogatory but which at the same time appropriately acknowledge the reasons why the child is unable to remain with their birth family.

When children worry about being removed

In some situations children may worry that contact with their birth family may result in the birth family removing the child from their permanent family. This may be particularly so if the child has lived with foster carers in the past and has experienced returns home which have been unsuccessful. It is important that everyone recognises this as a possible worry for the child and creates situations in which the child is able to express their concerns. For children with learning disabilities or communication difficulties, these opportunities are probably even more important.

Role-play can be an effective way of helping a child to understand their situation and recognise that they are now a permanent member of their new family and cannot be removed from them. In addition, adopters and permanent foster carers can also be offered support to think about the type of language they use around contact. They should be helped to think about using terminology which reassures the child that contact is something important but temporary and that the child will remain with their permanent family afterwards.

The following example, taken from Catherine Macaskill's chapter on managing contact arrangements for children with learning difficulties, from *Staying Connected* (Argent, 2002) explains how adopters coped with their disabled four-year-old's reaction to a contact visit from his birth parents.

Later that night after they had left, Karl screamed and screamed for several hours. Nothing could

> *console him. With his limited repertoire of language he was eventually able to demonstrate to his adopters that he was terrified that his birth parents were planning to steal him. His adopters role-played this scenario with him: Mummy Rosemary come to say 'Hi' to stay a little while, and then say 'Bye, bye Karl'. Acting out this real situation over and over again helped Karl to grasp what was happening.*

The issue of whether it is appropriate for younger children to have contact visits without members of their permanent family present is addressed elsewhere in this book. However, it is important to ensure that a child who has concerns about being returned to their birth family knows that their permanent family will be with them during the visit or will, at the very least, be present to accompany them to and from the visit.

When birth families fail to meet children's expectations

Children may develop a rosy picture of their birth family when they are no longer living with them. Meeting with them again may be a harsh reminder of the way a birth parent constantly overlooked them and favoured their siblings, or failed to protect them from an abusive partner. By encouraging permanent families and workers to maintain a non-judgemental but realistic view of the child's birth family, children can be helped to keep in mind both the positives and negatives of their experiences with their birth family.

Providing opportunities for children to express their feelings and validate their concerns will help them recognise the complexity of their feelings. For example, open questions such as, 'Do you remember what it was like when you went to stay with your foster carers?' can open up opportunities for children to talk about a birth parent's illness and why they could not live at home. Acknowledgements such as, 'I know you worried about your birth mum and found it hard when she left to look after your brother' give the child permission to express their mixed feelings about birth family situations.

> *My mum's not a motherly person. I wish she was but she's not but I like to see her. I enjoy our days out together as friends.*
>
> (A teenager who saw her birth mother twice a year, quoted in 'Contact Issues and Arrangements' in the guidance notes to 'Nutmeg Gets a Letter' (Foxon, 2003))

When birth families fail to write or attend meetings

A child or young person may be severely disappointed when a birth parent fails to attend a contact session, or may find it impossible to understand how they could fail to send them a birthday card on time. This may augment the anger and sadness the child already has about why their birth parents did not love them enough to give up a drug or alcohol habit, or failed to protect them from abuse.

Helping children to develop an age-appropriate understanding of the difficulties their birth family may be facing can lessen the distress when birth families appear to "let them down". Something as simple as encouraging the child to list all the tasks a parent has to do may help the child to recognise why their birth parent was not able to do these things for them. In any discussion with the child it is important to encourage them to appreciate that it is still OK for them to continue to love their birth family. There may also be ways of helping a child who is capable of making relevant connections to think about times when they have forgotten to do something, which does not in any way impact on their feelings about the people involved. Adopters and permanent foster carers may also want to make extra efforts to reassure the child about how much they are loved and valued by their new family, so that the child can maintain a sense of security and acceptance to help them cope with more distressing emotions.

> *We have to pick up the pieces when John's mother promises him impossible things. He now uses her for material gain.*
>
> *(An adopter, quoted in 'Contact in Adoption and Permanent Foster Care' (Neil and Howe, 2005))*

When a new child is born into the birth family or other siblings return home

It can be hard for a child to cope with the news that their birth parent has a new baby, or to discover that brothers and sisters have returned home when they cannot. Emotions may range from deep concern about their birth family's ability to properly care for the new baby or for the returning siblings, to strong feelings of anger and distress about their birth family's inability to care for them when they are able to care for other children. Children may find it difficult to control their feelings and will probably act them out within their new family. Permanent families may need help with supporting the child and answering difficult questions about the welfare of siblings.

Be open to the child's communication

When preparing or supporting children through contact, it is essential to keep the child's needs to the forefront. What is the child trying to communicate? Are they dropping hints about distress which they cannot voice, through their behaviour or passing comments? Are adults overlooking the child's risk of being severely traumatised or even re-abused because of their conviction that the benefits of contact will outweigh the child's sense of distress?

Workers may find themselves at risk of underplaying the concerns of permanent families who feel that the child is finding contact too distressing. If you are in this position, remind yourself of the reasons why the child has come into care. Remind yourself that the permanent family lives with the child on a day-to-day basis and sees the impact of contact in a way that you will never experience. They are probably better placed than anyone else to distinguish between the child feeling renewed grief for the loss of their family and the reawakening of old terrors linked to abuse and neglect. If they did not have such concern for the child's wellbeing, would you want them to care for this child in the first place?

TIP 7

Prepare and support adopters, foster carers and birth families

Jamaal has contact with his family twice a year. Some foster carers have really good relationships with their foster child's birth parents, but I think it is difficult for birth parents when they see their child doing well with someone else. They see Jamaal is a changed boy and they probably feel they have failed and wonder why couldn't they do the things we have done. I'm sure it is difficult for them and I don't blame them for not feeling comfortable with us. I think maybe I was just lucky to have these skills to

> *look after disabled children, and the training from Barnardo's enhanced that.*
>
> (Jabeen, the long-term carer of a boy with learning disabilities and behavioural problems, quoted in 'If you don't stick with me, who will?' (Bond, 2005))

Effective contact doesn't just happen – it needs careful preparation. Permanent families and birth relatives need opportunities to think through the aims of contact and to understand their role within it. They also need a chance to express their fears and aspirations and to consider how they can avoid or minimise difficult situations.

This support should remain available until the child reaches adulthood. Children, young people, adopters, permanent foster carers and birth relatives should all be able to access support, especially at "transitional" times in the child's life, such as the move to secondary school. Other parties may also need access to support, for example, the temporary foster family caring for the siblings of a child placed for adoption, where there are issues around contact.

Preparing and supporting black and minority ethnic families

> *After spending the first part of my life in a predominantly white environment, being placed with a black family was the most significant move for me. Before this I was confused about who I was and not at all confident about my culture. Through regular contact with key members of my family, I then learned truly to value my heritage. Knowing who you are and where you come from is very important because without it you cannot plan for the future.*
>
> (Zena Dickson, who was previously in care, quoted in 'See you Soon' (Argent, 1995))

51

It is widely acknowledged that black families tend to be more open to the idea of children being cared for outside their immediate family. However, this is no reason to assume that all black and minority ethnic families will be open to the idea of contact or will need less support to manage contact. Families from black and minority ethnic communities may have experienced racism or be especially wary of contact with authorities, and may be less willing to admit to problems or seek help when they occur. Unless you make it apparent that support is readily and constantly available to all parties involved in adoption, these families may not come forward to ask for it.

You may also want to ensure that you can provide support from a source which is clearly seen as independent from the placing or assessment agency. Families may appreciate support from a worker who reflects their ethnicity and has knowledge of their culture, language and religion. However, this won't always be the case and some families living in areas where there are, for example, very few other Bangladeshi families may have serious concerns about receiving support from another Bangladeshi worker for reasons of confidentiality. It is best not to make assumptions in these cases but to find out what families would prefer – when a choice is available.

Don't assume contact will work well in kinship placements

It is sometimes assumed that contact will be more successful in situations where children are permanently placed with family relatives. Whilst this may be true in some cases, this viewpoint can also ignore the fact that families often have their own personality clashes and differences of opinion. An aunt looking after her sister's child, or a grandparent caring for her grandchild may feel very angry with the parent who has failed to care for the child. The birth parents may in turn resent relatives who they believe have taken the "side" of social services against them.

Another issue which can occur within kinship placements relates to how the carers can protect children from abusive relatives or partners of relatives. Whereas it may be quite straightforward for an adopter or foster carer to exclude a specific person from contact arrangements, it may be difficult for a kinship carer to preclude all contact with a relative or partner of a relative who is present at family gatherings or who may arrive whilst the carer and child are visiting other relatives' homes.

For all these reasons, kinship carers should be offered the same level of support and access to outside help which is offered to other adopters and long-term carers.

Prepare all parties for contact

The extra time spent helping all parties to prepare for contact will pay dividends in the long run. If initial contact experiences are positive ones, then permanent families and birth families are more likely to want to remain engaged with the process, and the establishment of good practice at an early stage creates a helpful framework for future contact.

Clarifying simple issues like which family writes first, or when phone calls will be made to set up face-to-face meetings, can avoid stress and misunderstanding in the long term.

Workers will be best placed to help all parties prepare for the renewal of contact after a break, if they have a holistic view of the situation. For example, if they have recently met with the birth relatives, they can prepare the child and adopters for the fact that the birth mother has changed the length, style and colour of her hair and looks very different. Similarly, they can prepare the birth family for the reality that the "child" is now a teenager and has swapped their love of trains for a passion for dance music.

Preparation starts before the contact process begins

In previous chapters we looked at the idea that preparation for contact begins when people apply to become adopters or foster carers. With this foundation of understanding about the value of contact to children and their identity development, it will be easier to support permanent families in negotiating the actual process of establishing and maintaining contact.

In a similar way, birth relatives can also contribute towards creating a sound basis for successful contact. For example, a birth mother can be supported to create a life story book for the child to take to their new family.

Prepare adoptive or permanent foster families for exchanging information indirectly

> *The first letter, I didn't know what it was about because I was about four. And when I was six...the letter I got from her, I started crying because my mum explained it all to me...It is a nice feeling that she is actually able to contact me. 'Cause I feel, I still feel part of her if you know what I mean, I still feel that she is my mum and that, she, she still loves me because at the bottom of letters, its say 'love from your dear mum'.*
>
> (*A ten-year old boy speaking about indirect contact with his mother, quoted in 'Contact in Adoption and Permanent Foster Care' (Neil and Howe, 2004)*)

- Even if contact is to be indirect, there can be huge benefits from adopters meeting with birth family members before or soon after the child is placed. This can help adopters to acquire more understanding of the birth family, and possibly empathy for their situation. It will also enable the adopters to answer their child's questions about their birth family, and maybe to develop a better understanding of the child's feelings about them. Also, writing to people you have met is easier than corresponding with complete strangers, and will help the adoptive or foster family to get the best out of indirect contact, for the child's benefit.
- Some birth families may find it too painful to meet adopters at the time of placement but may find it easier to do this after some time has elapsed. The opportunity for meeting "later on" should not be discounted if birth families refuse early requests for a meeting.
- Don't assume that adopters and permanent carers will know how to write the type of letter required, or find it easy to do so. Provide guidance on letter writing and issues such as how to safeguard confidentiality. Adopters often speak of worrying whether it is OK to mention aspects of the child's life, like family holidays, because

they are aware of the financial gulf between the birth family's life and their own.

- Offer support to adopters and foster carers who are writing to birth relatives with learning disabilities to ensure they have information on how best to approach this, or can consider more appropriate ways of communicating with someone who has literacy difficulties.

- Encourage birth families to consider what sort of information the child would like to gain through contact. How can they ascertain this without raising expectations in the child which may not be met? How can they phrase letters in ways which will elicit the sort of responses the child will find helpful?

- Help adopters and permanent carers of children with disabilities to find ways that the child can participate in exchanging information, for example, involving the child in selecting postcards and photographs to send.

- Help adopters and permanent carers to think about the type of information birth relatives might like to receive. What will reassure them that the child is well and happy? What milestones in the child's life are likely to be important to them? Offer ideas and suggestions for ways in which the permanent family can put together a package of materials to send to the birth family, for example, writing a card from a day out, taking photos at the school play and keeping children's paintings to include in the next communication.

Prepare birth families for exchanging information "indirectly"

I tried to sit down a couple of times and write a letter to them so it could be put in the file for when they reach of age and I just couldn't do it...It hurt too much to put my feelings down on paper. It still does.

(Birth mother with one way letterbox contact, quoted in 'Contact in Adoption and Permanent Foster Care' (Neil and Howe, 2004))

- Birth relatives may need guidance about how to structure a letter and the type of information to include. How will you provide this, particularly if the person is already struggling with literacy? Can you provide this support through a tape or over the phone?
- Birth families may need help with actually writing the letter. Will speaking onto a tape or making a video be more natural and easier for some birth families?
- Can you provide interpreters or translators to support birth families for whom English is not their first language?
- Birth families may need help to think about the type of information which will benefit rather than distress the child.
- Birth families may need help to think about how they will address the child and how this will impact on them. For example, a letter signed 'Mum Karen' will be less confusing and distressing for the child than a letter signed 'Your only and ever loving Mum'.
- Will it be easier if the birth family has something to respond to, for example, if the adoptive or permanent carers write first?
- How can you help birth relatives to recognise that the child is growing up and that their tastes and interests may change relatively quickly?
- How can you help birth families to understand that children's views may change as they get older? The young child who is excited about sending paintings and photos to birth relatives may become, as a teenager, very resentful about having information conveyed about their life to people they feel they hardly know.

Prepare adopters and foster carers for face-to-face meetings

- It is important to help adopters and permanent carers to recognise that contact meetings are not a test of the birth family's ability to relate to the child. Encourage adopters and long-term foster carers to recognise their own skills and the useful role they can play in empowering birth families to make contact as beneficial as possible for the child.
- It may be helpful for permanent families and birth relatives to meet together for the first time without the child, or at least to have a phone conversation. Coming together to create the contact agreement may be a good opportunity for birth relatives and

permanent families to meet, but in some cases a separate meeting may be needed to give both families an opportunity to talk in a more informal setting.

- Don't assume that just because adopters and permanent carers have managed indirect contact successfully with the child's birth family over a lengthy period that they will adapt easily to the introduction of face-to-face contact. Extra support or even therapeutic input may be required to prepare and support families for direct contact.

- Offer permanent families opportunities to role-play difficult situations which they believe may occur during contact or to explore the best way to approach sensitive questions they want to ask the birth family.

- Consider how you can help adopters and permanent carers manage their feelings about birth families which they believe have seriously harmed their child. It can be very difficult for a family caring for a child who has been seriously disabled by neglect or mistreatment in the birth family, or damaged in the womb by the mother's alcohol or drug misuse, to keep their anger from impacting negatively during contact. They have probably seen the child undergoing painful medical treatment or being limited, on a daily basis, from enjoying experiences their peers take for granted and may find it hard to forgive the birth family for causing this.

- Be clear about what support will be available during or after contact.

Prepare birth families for face-to-face contact

We've had some fun with him. We've watched him grow up. Not on a photograph. We've felt him grow up. We've tapped him on the head. I've stood next to him now where he is almost up to my shoulder and he's been looking at me and said, 'It won't be long till I'm taller than you'.

(Grandmother speaking about face-to-face contact, quoted in 'Contact in Adoption and Permanent Foster Care' (Neil and Howe, 2004))

- If there has been a considerable period of indirect contact before a face-to-face meeting, additional support may be needed to prepare birth relatives for this. In some cases therapeutic input may be desirable.

- Help birth families who have not seen the child since infancy to understand that the child will not immediately "recognise" them. Children may need to develop a relationship from scratch with birth relatives they have no memory of.

- Encourage birth relatives not to expect too much from the child and to try and find ways to interact naturally with them. A child may not want to be cuddled by or sit on the knee of someone they don't know well, but may be happy to play on the swings with them.

- Make it clear who is included in the contact arrangements and make birth relatives aware that having too many people present can be overwhelming for the child. Ensure they are aware of anyone who is not allowed to attend contact.

- Help birth relatives to prepare for the possibility that a child with severe disabilities may have declined in health or ability since they last saw them. Also prepare them for the fact that the permanent family may see something as "progress" which the birth family may feel is simply an indication of the child's low developmental level. They may also need practical advice about how to handle or interact with a disabled child.

- Help birth families to think through and identify any potentially difficult questions which the child may ask. How will they cope with this? Will they all give the same answer?

- Be clear about what support will be available during or after contact.

The social worker asked me how I feel meeting them and I told her I was nervous. Not worried about what was going to happen, but worried about what they were going to be like, how [my son] was going to react, what to call him.

(Birth mother who had help from her social worker to prepare for her first contact meeting, quoted in 'Staying Connected' (Argent, 2002))

When to offer supervision

In the early stages of establishing contact there may be many uncertainties and insecurities between permanent families and birth families. Tensions may arise purely from the stresses these cause which may be harmful to the long-term success of contact. For this reason, it can be beneficial to offer supervision to participants during early face-to-face meetings. Once all participants feel more secure and relaxed in their relationship, this supervision may no longer be required. Some contact may always need supervision to ensure that a child is not frightened by or placed at risk by erratic behaviour, for example, from a non-abusive parent who is affected by mental health issues which may be difficult for adopters and children to handle. (In the following chapter, the benefits of using a specialist setting for some types of contact visit are outlined.)

Good supervision during contact is open and supportive and aims to facilitate rather than to control or direct, but is ready to intervene when issues occur and help participants to reach solutions.

Recognise individual strengths and support vulnerabilities

Some adopters and permanent carers will be very empathic to the needs of birth relatives. This empathy can lead to the development of a productive relationship which will make contact highly beneficial for the child. In such situations, adopters may decide to forgo the services of an intermediary and make all their own arrangements directly with the birth family. If this happens – especially if this is against the advice of your agency – it may be instinctive to want to withdraw support and "let the family get on with it". However, it is much more useful to let the adopters and the birth family know that your agency, or the independent service you provide, is still available for them if they need help in the future. This is important for many reasons, not least of which is the fact that some adopters and permanent carers may find themselves becoming overwhelmed by the needs and problems of the birth family. They may need support and intervention to help them re-negotiate this relationship with the birth family so that it stays within manageable boundaries and does not detract from the time and energy available for the child.

Provide support after contact

Contact is part of an ongoing process which enables the child to piece together their history and connections with their birth family. Therefore, it is not surprising that the sum of the whole may often be much more successful than the individual parts. As discussed in the previous chapter, a child may appear very distressed and disturbed by contact and their behaviour may cause adopters and foster carers to question whether contact is upsetting rather than helping the child. How will you ensure that the adopters have a chance to explore the reasons behind this? How will you ensure that adopters and permanent carers are able to voice these concerns without feeling that they will be criticised for being opposed to the idea of contact?

Birth relatives may also need support after contact. Will someone be on-hand to accompany the distressed birth mother who leaves face-to-face contact alone? Will someone be in touch a few days later to see if she needs additional support? Will someone work with the grandparent who cannot understand why their grandson no longer wants to cuddle them and is upset when they talk about how much the child is missed by their siblings? For birth parents of children with disabilities, contact may generate feelings of inadequacy about their inability to care for the child which they may contrast with the evident abilities of the adoptive family.

> *I was in tears. So she [social worker] actually stood there and gave me a cuddle and talked to me about it and then walked me back to the car and then left. Lucky she was there.*
>
> *(Birth mother, speaking about the support her social worker gave her to cope with the ending of her first contact meeting, quoted in 'Staying Connected' (Argent, 2002))*

Contact may raise major issues for a birth parent on many levels and they may need opportunities to express their feelings or to think through the impact of their behaviour on the child. In some cases, contact may trigger major issues from a birth relative's own life and they may need professional help to address these.

TIP 8

Choose venues and activities carefully

You know, it is more flexible now and both sides admit it is easier and it was a better meeting. And it is a nicer meeting as well because you don't mind, you know, if you are going to go to the zoo, or you are going to go here, because you know the kids are going to enjoy themselves anyway and we are going to enjoy ourselves as well...I mean, when we come back, when we have had the contact, in past contacts you have come away from it and you think, 'Well, that was OK and that is over for another year', sort of thing, but I mean this last one was so much more relaxed...We came back and said, 'Well, wasn't that lovely, that was a really nice meeting'.

(Adoptive father talking about how his daughter's birth family had agreed to contact taking place at a family pub with a children's play area, quoted in 'Contact in Adoption and Permanent Foster Care' (Neil and Howe, 2004))

Face-to-face contact is often an emotionally-charged time for everyone involved. Aim to create an experience which minimises the tension and distress so that the positive aspects can come to the fore.

- Create an experience which will reinforce the child's sense of security and belonging in their permanent family.
- Ensure that the child does not feel "abandoned" to a previously distressing or abusive situation, which may cause them to question their permanent family's ability to protect them from harm.
- Do not recreate difficult memories from the past of previous less pleasant experiences by avoiding venues which have negative associations.
- Provide an activity where the child will be relaxed and entertained so that birth relatives will find it easier to interact with them.
- Compile a list of suitable venues for adopters and other participants arranging contact. You should offer advice about the advantages and disadvantages of different venues, such as cost and safety implications and whether there is good disabled access. Also bear in mind that some adopters may want to choose venues which are closer to, or halfway between, their home and the birth family home.

Weigh up the options around different venues

Bear the following issues in mind when deciding on the best venue.

- A venue which keeps children occupied and provides adults with natural ways of interacting with the child – and also with each other – is likely to prove more successful than an environment where everyone sits around and looks at each other.
- If contact takes place in the adopter's or carer's home or in a neutral venue such as a family centre, it is important to ensure that there are plenty of games and activities to occupy the child

and prevent birth relatives from feeling awkward or under scrutiny.

- If necessary, ensure that there are facilities available to support the needs of a child or adult with severe physical disabilities.

- A visit to a swimming pool or anywhere with shared changing rooms should be avoided if sexual abuse is known or suspected to have taken place within the birth family.

- Have the cultural, religious and dietary needs of the different participants been considered? What about the needs of other children from the adoptive family or the birth children of families fostering the child's siblings?

- Some support workers recommend avoiding mealtimes as they feel cultural differences, memories stirred up by mealtimes and issues such as eating disorders may create unnecessary tensions. However, other workers acknowledge that some children and families feel relaxed in the familiar environment of a favourite restaurant and may find this the most comfortable place to meet. Encourage whoever is arranging the contact venue to think through the possible pros and cons of a particular option and ascertain whether it will meet the needs of everyone involved.

- The cost implications of venues need to be borne in mind. Will adopters choose venues which are beyond the financial means of the birth family or the foster family where siblings are living? If adopters offer to pay for birth relatives, will this lead to situations where the birth relatives feel embarrassed or indebted to the adoptive family? Will resentments arise on both sides if one party feels manipulated by the other? Can the agency contribute towards the cost of contact visits?

- If cost is a problem, the local authority adoption support service should be able to provide money to assist with this. In exceptional circumstances it might be acceptable for the adopters to subsidise the birth family for one contact visit during the year if a low or no-cost venue is chosen for the second visit.

- Have you allowed a sufficient budget to enable siblings and other birth relatives to maintain contact? Being unable to find someone to take them or to afford travel costs is one of the main reasons siblings cite for not seeing as much of each other as they would like.

- Do not rule out the possibility of contact taking place in the homes of birth relatives. However, this is something which may need to be thought about carefully and only included once good relationships have been established, and permanent families feel confident that children will not be exposed to risks. For older children who, for example, are used to regular visits to their grandparents' house, it may seem strange to cut these off altogether and you should offer support to permanent families to consider the implications.

Choose venues that suit the purpose of contact

> *I do miss him [my brother]. Sometimes I get desperate to see him...I used to get desperate to see him when I left him and sometimes it's quite upsetting, but I don't get that as much. I don't get that now...I do look forward to seeing him, but I don't, like, get desperate. I get used to it.*
>
> (A girl who has phone contact with her brother and sees him about three times a year, quoted in 'Adopted Children Speaking' (Thomas and Beckford with Lowe and Murch, 1999))

If face-to-face meetings are taking place, you need to consider which venues and activities will be most appropriate to meet the aims of the meeting. For example, if the aim is for a child to spend time getting to know their siblings, then playtime together in a park may be ideal for this, with the adopters and birth family joining in as they start to interact with each other. However, if the main aim is for adopters or permanent carers to discover more about the child's history and family connections (especially if there are concerns as to whether birth relatives will continue contact), then it may be essential to choose somewhere where the children can be safely occupied so that the adults can sit down together and have a more focused exchange of information.

Adopters may want to approach meetings and exchanges of information with a list of questions, and do some preparation work around how they will best be able to raise them. However, in any situation it is essential that thought is still given to what role the child will play in this. A child who sits bored and miserable while the adopters ply the birth grandmother with questions will not take away happy memories of the occasion. Such an experience may colour the child's perception of contact and have lasting repercussions for its usefulness in their lives.

How neutral is a neutral venue?

If you are choosing a "neutral" venue, consider just how "neutral" this will feel to the child. Returning to the family centre or a social services location which was used while the child was in a temporary placement might re-awaken painful memories which will overshadow the current purpose of contact.

Don't leave children feeling exposed

We place children in permanent families because we want them to have the opportunity to feel nurtured, protected and to have a sense of belonging. The aim of contact is to support the child's identity within this new environment and to minimise their sense of loss and the number of unanswered questions they have about their past. So why do we still come across examples of young children expected to travel alone in taxis to contact meetings, children being collected for contact visits by workers they have never met before?

If contact is taking place outside the permanent family's home or without the permanent carers present, you need to ensure that the child doesn't feel exposed to anxiety or possible abuse. Imagine what harm it can do to the child's trust in their permanent family's ability to care for and protect them, if at the most vulnerable times in their lives they are expected to handle events alone, or with just the support of an unfamiliar worker.

I had a one-month-old baby just detoxed from crack, a seven-year-old who was just lovely but she needed time...and they told me I had to "supervise" James and his mother...on my own. The gasman came to read the meter, the baby needed

> *changing...I had to leave James and his mum alone for a few minutes...it was then she told him that his dad would be coming to get him, which wasn't true.*
>
> (Experienced foster carer, quoted in 'Staying Connected' (Argent, 2002))

- How advisable is it to have contact visits for younger children where adopters and permanent carers are excluded?
- How can the child retain a sense of their permanent family's ability to protect them from harm if their permanent family are not present during the visit? For example, would it be better if their permanent foster carers drove them to the meeting and collected them afterwards?
- If no-one from their permanent family is present, who will ensure the child is not exposed to an abusive relative (whose behaviour is not known to social services) or becomes re-traumatised by inappropriate behaviour?
- Who knows the child well enough to pick up subtle aspects of their behaviour which convey distress?
- Who knows the child's history well enough to discuss with them any aspects of their past where the birth family's version of events may clash with the child's own memories?
- Who will be able to brief the permanent family in detail about what the child has experienced during the contact visit, so that the permanent family can best decide how to handle any repercussions from this?

If it is decided that it is really not appropriate or possible for the permanent family to be present during a contact visit and a worker is to accompany the child instead, then it is important that this person establishes a relationship with the child prior to the visit. This person must know and be known by the child well enough to provide a positive and reassuring "link" for the child with their permanent family. They should also know about the child's history and the reasons for their separation from their birth family, and be able to identify relevant issues to pass on to the permanent family.

Of course, older children and children who are established in their permanent family may choose to see their birth family alone and may have the emotional resources to handle this. They may want to go and stay in the birth family home or with other relatives. Some young people may wish to take over making their own arrangements for contact. Their permanent family may need to recognise when young people have reached this stage of independence, and be prepared to let them move towards this in appropriate stages.

Consider the need for safe care

It can be highly beneficial to introduce "safe care" guidelines to everyone prior to contact visits, with a careful explanation of how these can protect both the child and the adults from misunderstanding and misplaced allegations. Think about how you will ensure these guidelines are maintained and monitored during face-to-face contact.

Be clear about time limits

Quality is better than quantity in most cases, and clear time limits should be set for face-to-face contact. Everyone should be made aware of the timetable and enough time should be allowed so that visits can end as calmly as possible with a sense of closure for everyone involved. Allowing too much time to say goodbyes can create too much emotional impact which can be stressful for the child and the adults involved, but rushed goodbyes can also be equally emotional and unsatisfactory.

Permanent families may also need to be encouraged to use their discretion around timings for phone calls. Imposing a time limit may help a birth relative to use the time more productively to communicate with the child or young person, and may avoid situations where birth relatives may be tempted to download their problems onto the child.

Consider a specialist setting for contact

Rashid was four when he began having frequent supervised contact with his mother in a specialist setting prior to the full care order being made. Rashid would arrive for contact 'running with a beaming smile' into his mother's arms. Zahide [the mother], however, often behaved in a florid, hallucinatory and paranoid way. Supervision protected Rashid from the effects of this, while allowing him, over time, to begin distinguishing safely between his mother's behaviour and other, less troubled adults.

(Quoted in 'Staying Connected' (Argent, 2002))

There may be times when contact requires a very high level of supervision to make it a safe and beneficial experience. This may be particularly useful if:

- adopters and permanent foster carers feel they cannot provide the level of constant supervision needed to ensure the birth family does not say or do something to the child which will seriously undermine the child's stability in their new family;
- there are so many children and adults involved in the contact that it is difficult to ensure that sufficient supervision can be provided to ensure the safety of all the children;
- a birth parent has serious mental health problems and may need input from trained staff;
- Birth relatives have not accepted the permanent placement and do not understand the impact on the child of their attempts to undermine the placement;
- difficult and destructive behaviour from other children (or adults) may make it difficult to have contact in a public place or in the adopters' home;
- lack of safe, suitable venues is proving a major sticking point in the success of contact, which may lead to breakdown in the arrangements.

A specialist setting offers a home-from-home environment, with enough comfortable, private sitting rooms so that each family can have their own space. There are also kitchens for families to prepare and share meals, a plethora of activities to keep children occupied, and a garden where they can let off steam. The "homely" nature of the environment helps children and families to relax and also offers room for individuals to withdraw for a while, if they need time for themselves. One of the most beneficial aspects of the service is the presence of skilled and qualified staff who are able to intervene immediately and firmly if anything of concern occurs. Support is also provided to help participants resolve issues that arise and to improve the quality of the interaction. This can include providing mediation between different parties.

Time alone

For some children, time spent alone with birth relatives will not be desirable. However, for other children, a limited amount of time spent alone with their relatives may be very beneficial and may contribute to the development of a positive relationship. If adopters or permanent foster carers have strong concerns about the child being alone during contact with birth relatives, it is important to encourage them to voice these concerns. This can prove a useful starting point for them to identify the reasons behind their concerns and to recognise whether they are well founded or simply based on anxieties around the child forming or reforming strong attachments with birth relatives. Talking through their concerns can help permanent families to identify ways in which their concerns could be addressed or alleviated.

It can also be helpful for birth relatives to be made aware of permanent families' concerns. If birth relatives realise that their behaviour is having or is likely to have a negative impact on the child – which is causing concern for adopters – they may understand why it is important for them to modify their behaviour.

TIP 9

Keep the approach flexible and explore alternatives if things are not working out

If it becomes clear that contact is proving very distressing or is damaging the child's ability to settle into their permanent family, then contact may need to be stopped, significantly altered or conducted by a different means. Before making fundamental changes to the process – such as stopping contact altogether – it is important to consider what lies behind the problems and what scale of modifications will be needed to better meet the child's needs.

Issues in sibling contact

Whilst the benefits of sibling contact are widely recognised, this does not mean that all sibling contact will be a positive experience for all the children involved. In a minority of cases, contact with siblings may expose children to memories of abuse or recreate situations in which children were bullied and physically or sexually abused by one another. Where one sibling was ignored or neglected whilst others were favoured by a birth parent, meeting with the favoured siblings may be distressing for the less-favoured child. Similarly, older children who took on caring roles for their younger siblings may find it very hard to adjust to the fact that they are no longer required to assume this role. Children who see evidence that their siblings appear to be neglected or mistreated in the birth family may find direct contact more upsetting than beneficial.

Temporary breaks in face-to-face contact may allow children time to adjust to their new situations. Changing face-to-face contact for letterbox or telephone contact may allow a vulnerable child to grow up with a sense of connection with their siblings which does not expose them to harm. Face-to-face contact can then be reconsidered when children are more mature and better able to protect themselves or modify their behaviour. Ignoring an older child's concerns and wish for contact with their siblings can lead to a situation where the child feels compelled to leave the adoptive family in order to return to their birth family in order to care for younger children. However, it could also be argued that the older child who knows nothing about their siblings would not be put in this situation in the first place! The situation is a complex one and each child's case must be handled individually.

Does this suit the personalities involved?

We were told basically, in a nutshell, that if you didn't go for contact there would be less chance of getting a child. You will say anything and do anything at that stage.

(Adopter, quoted in 'Contact in Adoption and Permanent Foster Care' (Neil and Howe, 2004))

It is human nature to rebel against things which are imposed on us. So, if the process around contact feels too prescriptive, there may be times when adopters or birth families find themselves assuming an 'I'll show them' attitude by sabotaging the process. In addition, teenagers may be particularly anxious to "rebel" against something they feel is being dictated by an anonymous "system", not to mention their adopters, permanent carers or social workers!

Where contact arrangements are not working out, it is important to take the problem back to the people involved and seek their ideas for ways to make it work more effectively. Imposing more demands or starting to talk about enforcing contact through the court will not help the situation at this stage. It is, in any case, unlikely that a court will be willing to enforce an arrangement which goes against the wishes and better judgement of an otherwise excellent adopter or carer with a residence order. What punitive measures would the court resort to? Removing the child is unlikely to serve anyone's interests!

An adoptive family which believes that agency workers respect their knowledge of the child and their desire to protect them from harm are more likely to consider "keeping the door ajar" for contact to resume in future, even if they feel unhappy about engaging in contact at the present time.

Show trust in the permanent family

Some permanent families will only engage fully in contact when they feel able to "take over" the arrangements themselves. This may cause some initial concern for their workers but research shows that adopters who actively decide to manage their own contact arrangements are often well placed to make arrangements work successfully in ways which benefit both the child and the birth family.

> *I think if you put a block on something that someone wants to do they want to do it even more. I think it is important for Zoe to feel part of the [birth] family, you know, to get her niche with her sisters and brother...and I think she has, yes, she has. I know she has.*
>
> *(Adoptive mother who, with the support of her social worker, negotiated sleepovers for her daughter at the birth mother's house, quoted in 'Contact in Adoption and Permanent Foster Care' (Neil and Howe, 2004))*

Experienced foster carers and some skilled, or particularly empathic, adopters may recognise the birth family's discomfort with a mediated process and decide it is better to make their own arrangements directly with them. If you find yourself wanting to discourage this, you need to ask yourself why you feel this way. Are there genuine concerns about the child's safety which the permanent family is overlooking? If so, can you help them to recognise these and ensure that they are not putting the child at unnecessary risk? Or are you finding it hard to let go of the professional support role and empower the adopters to manage their own arrangements? Are there compromises you can put in place, such as offering regular reviews or providing help with specific aspects of contact?

Consider Family Group Conferences

Some of the problems of making contact work in kinship placements have been discussed in previous chapters, and it is essential to recognise that kinship placements may need the same level of support as placements with strangers. Again, the same principles apply around people being more committed to arrangements they have made themselves, and Family Group Conferences (FGCs) can be a very useful tool in this process. In a FGC a facilitator brings family members together (possibly including neighbours and close family), establishes ground rules for the process, and then leaves participants to find their own outcomes. The facilitator then rejoins the group for them to feed back their decisions and helps them to think through the implications of how these will work. Finally, the facilitator ensures that the family and anyone working with the child and family has copies of the agreement.

It may be necessary to offer support to help kinship carers, birth parents and other relatives to implement the decisions which have been identified during the FGC.

Be prepared to adjust arrangements

A bit of creative thinking and a change of venue or timescales may change the dynamics in a contact meeting. The example below shows how contact arrangements were adapted so that the needs of individual siblings could be addressed.

One [adoptive] family had agreed to meet twice a year with their children's older brothers. One older brother was well settled in foster care and very affectionate toward his younger brother and sister. The adopters described contact with him as 'a joy'. However, the other brother suffered from ADHD and had physically and emotionally abused his younger siblings, who were terrified of him. They pleaded not to see him but the local authority insisted on joint meetings with both brothers at an adoption party. Eventually the adopters came up with a compromise, so that the younger siblings met their oldest brother for lunch and play at a suitable pub, and they were joined by their older brother and his social worker prior to going out to a park. This worked better.

(Quoted in 'Nutmeg Gets a Letter: Practice guidelines'
(Foxon, 2003))

Signs which indicate that contact arrangements may need reviewing

Be aware of the signs which indicate that it may be time for contact arrangements to be reviewed. Do not be tempted to let situations under strain continue to run in the hope that things will somehow sort themselves out. In such cases, there is a risk that the situation may break down and permanent damage may be done to the relationships between the participants, which could make it almost impossible to renegotiate contact in the future. Signs include:

- the child displaying serious behaviour problems;
- children and young people asking for more/less contact or for contact with different people;
- the permanent family expressing concerns;
- the birth family expressing concerns;
- significant changes in the birth family circumstances;
- siblings returning to the birth family after a foster placement;
- a placement breaking down for one of the children involved in the contact arrangement;
- inappropriate information being passed on to children by the birth family during contact.

Stopping contact doesn't have to be permanent

If, after careful consideration, it is agreed that it is best to stop a particular type of contact, such as face-to-face meetings, this should not be seen as a permanent arrangement. Instead it should be seen as a "suspension" of contact which will be reviewed in the future. The pre-school child who finds it too painful to meet with his mother because of the memories this stirs up of her inability to protect him from abuse may be in a better position to cope with this contact in their early teens. Indeed, by that age he may be actively seeking contact in order to seek questions about his past and sense of identity.

When contact is suspended, it is important that reasons are clearly given to all the parties involved. Without explanations children may believe that the suspension is because they have done something wrong, or they may wonder if they will ever see their birth relatives again. If contact has been stopped because of distress expressed by the child, it can be empowering for the child to realise that their feelings have been responded to. It is also important to reassure the child that situations may change and that just because they cannot meet certain relatives in the immediate future, this is not necessarily a permanent arrangement.

Support should be offered to help birth relatives cope with this decision and maybe reach some understanding of how their behaviour may have contributed to this. For example, the birth mother who cannot accept why her child is distressed by them bringing along their latest partner to contact meetings may not have taken on board the reality of their previous partner having abused the child. This birth mother may need help to understand that although the child still loves her, the child does not trust in her ability to protect them from harm.

Where face-to-face contact is suspended, adopters and permanent foster carers should be encouraged to "keep the door open" by continuing some form of information exchange with the birth family. Even if the birth family chooses not to respond, the information can be stored by an intermediary service, so they can access it when they feel able to do so.

Marking the end of face-to-face contact

Many agencies hold what is colloquially referred to as a "goodbye " or a "wishing you well" visit to mark the end of direct contact between a child and their birth family. This is often when the child is placed for adoption and indirect contact is the plan, but these visits may also be used if direct contact is stopped at some point during the permanent placement.

These meetings can be extremely painful for birth relatives and for children old enough to realise the significance of saying "goodbye" until a point when in adulthood they may (or may not) choose to resume face-to-face contact. Some people view these meetings as a positive way of "keeping the doors open" by marking the start of indirect contact, while others worry that calling them names like "goodbye meetings" gives a message that there will never be face-to-face contact in the future. However, the alternative is to allow the contact to lapse without warning, which can be even more distressing for those involved.

Birth families will need a great deal of support to help them prepare for and cope with these meetings. Some birth relatives may find it too painful and disappear from the process.

Children will also need help to cope with this transition to a different form of contact. Older children may need support to understand that, while the possibility of seeing their family when they are older remains, there will be no face-to-face contact for the foreseeable future. Siblings may be grieving and will need explanations and support. Adopters may need support to help them think about how they will handle children's concerns about birth relatives becoming ill or dying before they have a chance to see them again.

TIP 10

Keep contact alive by offering ongoing support

I'm totally for contact, but it is quite exhausting because there is a lot to do, all the arranging and then dealing with the aftermath in his emotions and then worrying about the emblem on his school jumper and all sorts of things which make it quite complicated.

(Adoptive parent, quoted in 'Contact in Adoption and Permanent Foster Care' (Neil and Howe, 2004))

Don't assume that contact will run itself; that once you've got everyone agreed to the process and seen them through the complexities of the first episode of contact, that everything will then run smoothly until the child reaches adulthood. If children are to benefit from contact then contact must be flexible. It must adapt to the changing needs of the growing child and to the ups and downs of family life in both the child's birth family and permanent family.

Contact is a three-way process and unless all parties feel engaged and committed to making it work, the child's needs may be lost beneath the tensions and emotional struggles. The best way of offering support to the parties involved in contact is to ensure that everyone feels valued – both in their relationship to the child but also in terms of having a valuable role to play in making contact work.

Where, when and how should support be provided?

Support is most useful when it is clearly identified and when permanent families and birth families feel they can call upon it whenever help is needed. In addition, it is highly beneficial if support services can be pro-active – making contact with different parties to see how they can offer support, and finding out if they need help before a crisis point is reached.

Good practice dictates that support should be available:

- to help different parties prepare for contact;
- during contact (in certain circumstances);
- after contact for de-briefing, and, in some cases, comfort and reassurance (especially for distressed birth parents);
- to support permanent families dealing with children's resulting behaviour;
- to help re-negotiate contact at relevant times and if problems occur;
- to take account of children and young people's changing needs;
- when one form of contact ends or another starts.

At this time Joanne, who was now 15, started speaking about finding her dad, who it seemed had just disappeared off the face of the earth. She'd always spoken about her father as if he was someone in the past, but now she started to talk about him in the present...Then her dad was found dead. One of the dad's sisters rang up and painted a very rosy picture of him. Joanne had never heard good things about her dad before. I think Joanne was in shock. She was thinking about the fact that she would never get to see him. I have two relatives whose dad had died without them seeing him. I suggested that Joanne might like to talk to them about how they'd coped with this.

We went to the funeral and met some of the relatives she'd never known...Then we met Joanne's other sister – the sister she didn't know she had!...And all the relatives had nice stories to tell Joanne about her dad. Before that, all Joanne had was memories of her dad beating up her mum, and how much her nana hated her dad.

(Therese, foster carer, talking about the role that renewing links with the past played in the life of a teenager who she prepared for independent living, quoted in 'If you don't stick with me, who will?' (Bond, 2005))

Who should offer support?

Some birth relatives will find it very hard to work with staff from an agency they feel is responsible for the removal of their child. It may be more sensitive to offer support through an independent agency which the birth relatives consider to be neutral and open to listening to their feelings and point of view. However, every case is different and some birth relatives may have developed a strong bond with their existing social worker and may feel this person is best placed to understand and support them through painful times. You need to bear in mind that workers leave – no one stays in a job for ever! Who will hold the information this worker has acquired about a child and their two families? Who will take responsibility for getting in touch in the future to see how contact is going and whether anyone needs support? Who will be involved in a review of contact arrangements?

When these responsibilities rest within a specific service – perhaps contracted by the placing agency or an independent service within social services – these tasks will form part of that service's day-to-day work. If you don't have access to such a service, how can you create these processes within the existing structure of your agency? Do you have systems in place to collect and record information which will enable your agency to offer ongoing support to participants in contact? Too often valuable information leaves the agency when a particular member of staff leaves. Having up-to-date details of family circumstances and knowing what has worked or caused difficulties for participants in individual contact situations in the past can be very useful when providing future support.

Offer reviews as matter of course – not just when problems occur

> *I'd like to know more about my family. I found out quite a lot from her, and it makes me feel like I want to see other people that I hadn't heard of before.*
>
> *(A girl who had received news of her birth father through a female relative, quoted in 'Adopted Children Speaking' (Thomas and Beckford with Lowe and Murch, 1999))*

Contact arrangements should not be seen as something static, to be adjusted only when something goes wrong, but as a process which needs reviewing as the child grows older. Reviews should be offered as a matter of course, possibly planned around key transition periods in the child's life. Even successful arrangements will benefit from some rethinking, and children may be ready to see relatives who they did not feel so comfortable about meeting when they were younger. Build in a review process and don't wait for arrangements to start to show strain before you offer a review.

Work to maintain the parental status of birth parents

Knowing that someone else has become the "parent" to your child is very hard for birth parents to cope with. When a birth parent feels that their role in the child's life has been obliterated, they are much less likely to want to participate positively in contact. It is therefore important to help birth families maintain a sense of their role as a parent – albeit a changed or restricted one. Look for ways in which support services can reinforce this sense of parenthood and keep birth parents committed to wanting positive outcomes for the child, through contact and other aspects of the child's life. Help adopters and permanent foster carers recognise the importance of enabling birth parents to share some sense of this parental role – and the positive affects this will have for the child. Help them think about ways in which they can reinforce this sense of parental role for the birth parents.

Don't overlook support for sibling contact

Sometimes I go and see them [siblings], but social services all of a sudden stopped us and wouldn't provide the transport. But when I was adopted they said they would provide the transport. But now all of a sudden they stopped it. So we have to provide some of it...

(Anna, whose contact with her siblings was restricted by the availability of local authority transport and was angry with social services, quoted in 'Adopted Children Speaking' (Thomas and Beckford with Lowe and Murch, 1999))

Sibling contact is often one of the most neglected areas when it comes to providing support. This is possibly because social workers assume that sibling contact is somehow "less difficult" than contact with adult birth relatives, or perhaps because siblings may be placed across several adoptive and foster families and workers assume that without birth relatives in the mix, these parties will work co-operatively together. The different personalities, cultures, values and financial situations of the adoptive or foster families may be overlooked, and issues such as geographical distances are often minimised.

Never assume that families managing sibling contact do not need help. They may need support in managing aspects of their relationship with the other foster carers or adopters involved in the arrangement. Sibling contact could raise issues and risk factors that families may find difficult to cope with. They may also need support with travel expenses and issues such as when and how children can be driven to meetings. Similarly, birth relatives may find themselves struggling with how to explain to siblings living within the family that their brothers and sisters are unable to return to live with them. The child living in the birth family may also find it hard to be unable to phone or see their siblings as often as they are used to.

Some children may also need support to help them adjust to their new role in relation to their siblings. An older brother or sister who has cared for the younger children through difficult times, or a child who has taken on responsibilities for a disabled sibling, may find it very difficult to adapt to "playing" with their sibling in a situation where an adult takes all the decisions.

You need to be as alert to the issues raised by sibling contact as any other type of contact, and prepared to offer support to all parties involved – the child and their permanent family, and children and adults in the birth family.

Recognise implications for confidentiality

When sibling contact is taking place, it is important to recognise that levels of confidentiality may be impossible to maintain. Children should not be expected to keep secrets from one another and cannot be expected to differentiate between what will or will not be an identifying factor for birth relatives. Also, there is always the possibility that a child who is living with foster carers may return home at some time. Workers need to support adopters and foster carers to accept this, and think through any possible consequences.

In cases of sibling contact, the deciding factor always has to be the needs of the individual child. If a birth parent poses a serious threat to the child then it may not be possible for the child to have direct contact with siblings living with the birth family or to return to the birth family.

Look for ways to support the process

Very simple things can help permanent carers to help their child or young person to get the best out of contact. For example, a child who is able to choose where photos of their birth siblings are displayed in their adoptive home may experience this as a very positive step toward integrating their sense of both families existing concurrently rather than in conflict. Provide ongoing training and information which helps permanent families to remain aware of the value of contact and to keep searching for ways to make it a truly meaningful experience for the child or young person.

Endpiece

As this guide was going to press, a report was published by A National Voice – the organisation run for and by children and young people who are care-experienced. Called *Brothers and Sisters Survey* (2007), it highlights the feelings of children and young people from care about their need for contact with birth siblings, and also with foster siblings (children of foster carers or other children fostered in the family).

The survey showed that, among the children and young people surveyed, 83 per cent of respondents who do not live with their birth siblings would like to see more of them and 38 per cent of respondents who did not live with their foster siblings would like to see more of them.

When asked what prevented them seeing as much of their siblings as they would like, the main reasons given by respondents were that their siblings lived too far away or that it cost too much to see them.

Some of the respondents clearly felt very disempowered in their situation.

I don't know where some of them are.

She might not want to meet me.

My youngest brother lives with my nan and we don't get on.

Others felt that obstructions were being put in their way.

My mum will not let me see them.

Social services get in the way.

My social worker doesn't let me see her.

Whilst it would be wrong to speculate on the individual situations which led to these comments, there is nonetheless a suggestion that some children and young people still feel that they have very little say in matters around contact, and have a sense of it being something which is controlled by other people.

Saddest of all is the comment made by one respondent, who said:

Many of my brothers and sisters have grown up without me and I do not feel that they know me.

This sums up more precisely than any guide why it is so important to "leave the door open" for children to have some form of contact with their siblings, and other key people in their lives.

On a more reassuring note, it is worth mentioning that social workers were reported to be the ones who gave the most help and support to children to keep in touch with their birth siblings (43 per cent).

Although this report was about children and young people who are living or have lived in foster care (rather than about adoption or specifically those in permanent foster placements), it is important to remember that many children come to permanency after a considerable period in foster care. They may also have brothers and sisters still in foster placements or living within birth families. They may have attachments from foster homes to the children of their foster carers and to other foster children they have lived alongside.

Recognising this complexity of relationships is crucial if we are going to get it right for permanently placed children. We need to remember that the bond between a brother and sister who have helped to take care of each other in the face of parental neglect or the friendship created between two foster siblings who recognised each other as kindred spirits may have been the most powerful and sustaining relationship in that child's early life. These relationships –

forged in times when the rest of the world seems an alien, uncaring place – may be incredibly valuable building blocks for that child's future development.

Surely we have a duty to nurture and value relationships which have sustained children through very difficult periods? If we disregard them as inconsequential, what messages do we give about the importance and safety of building relationships in the future? If the aim of contact is to encourage children to grow into healthy adults, then we need to recognise the value of past relationships and the benefits they have brought to the child. Even when ongoing contact is not possible, there is a duty to encourage children to remember and talk about relationships which have sustained them in the past.

Appendix 1

(Taken from *Staying Connected* (Argent, 2002, p 216–219)

This is a sample contact agreement relating to contact between a birth mother, Mary, and her son, John, aged ten. It makes reference to the birth mother's live-in partner, Paul, and her daughter, Karen, who remains with her. It gives an idea of the level of detail that is required and consequently the amount of negotiation that is necessary to create clear guidelines and set out expectations from the very beginning.

Contact Agreement for John
This Agreement is made in good faith by all those involved.
The best interests of John will be considered at all times.
This Contact Agreement refers to the arrangements between Mary, John's birth mother, and Peter and Val before and after they adopt John.
What sort of contact is agreed?

Indirect:

Peter and Val will send written information on John and a photograph in February of each year. This will be sent to Barnardo's Post Box and forwarded to Mary.

Val and Peter will send a birthday card they have chosen with John to Karen via the Barnardo's Post Box. This will be sent three weeks in advance so there is time for it to be redirected.

Peter and Val will let Mary know of any significant events in John's life and any serious illnesses he might have.

Mary can send Val and Peter information about herself and Karen in April of each year via the Barnardo's Post Box.

Mary can send a birthday and Christmas card to John via the Barnardo's Post Box. This should be signed from Mummy Mary, Karen and Paul. Should Mary no longer live with Paul or Karen, then she should sign the card from Mummy Mary.

Mary will let Peter and Val know via the Post Box of any significant changes in her life.

Mary will keep Barnardo's informed of any change of address.

Direct:

Peter and Val will take John to Mary, once a year, to spend time at an activity based around Colchester. The meeting will last for approximately two hours and Peter or Val will be present throughout.

Whilst Mary continues to live with Paul, he will be welcome to attend along with Karen. There should be no other family members at this contact.

Arrangements for the contact will be made via Barnardo's Post Adoption Worker. It is anticipated that contact will usually be in the summer holiday at a date to be agreed by all the parties.

What role will the agency's Post Adoption/Post Placemenet Service play?

Negotiate the Agreement.

Circulate the Agreement to all the parties.

Be available for support and advise over any aspect of the contact.

Arrange the venue and date of direct contact on an annual basis.

Re-negotiate Agreements.

Provide information and review the Agreement as specified.

Agreement

I/we agree to the contact described above.

I/we agree that all actions and plans must be in the best interests of John and consistent with his wishes and feelings.

I/we agree to inform the agency of any change of address.

I/we agree to respect John's wishes should he want to change the terms of this Agreement at any time.

This Agreement will be reviewed after three years.

Signed_____Date_____John

Signed_____Date_____Mary

Signed_____Date_____Paul

Signed_____Date_____Peter

Signed_____Date_____Val

Signed_____Date_____BNFP*

Signed_____Date_____LA**

(Reproduced with thanks to Jackie Trent and Colchester New Families Project)

* Barnardo's New Families Project
** Local authority

Appendix 2

This is a précis of the contact arrangements currently used by The Berkshire Information Exchange Service, which is operated by The Berkshire Adoption Advisory Service. (A more detailed description of this service appears in 'Through the letterbox', by Alison Vincent and Alyson Graham, which appears as Chapter 4 of *Staying Connected* (Argent, 2002).) This has been reproduced with permission from Alison Vincent and Alyson Graham at the Berkshire Information Exchange Service.

The structure of the service

The Berkshire Information Exchange was established in 1994.

There are 421 active letterbox exchanges and the service facilitates over 1,200 exchanges per year (as of May 2007).

The Letterbox Co-ordinator is a qualified social worker with many years' experience in the field of adoption and fostering. This post is supported by an administrator.

The service aims to be "independent" in order to make it more approachable and less intimidating to all parties. It also recognises that court processes may have created an adversarial relationship between the birth family and the local authority.

The service is underpinned by written guidelines for workers, adopters and birth family members. This includes contact arrangement forms and guidance for letter writing.

Training on the Information Exchange and contact issues in general is included in adopters' preparation groups.

Workers are also offered training on the role of the Information Exchange.

Work on the detailed arrangements for indirect contact is usually completed by the link worker for the adopters and the worker for the child. The role of these workers is considered pivotal in the future functioning of the service.

The Letterbox Co-ordinator can be called upon for advice and mediation during these initial arrangements. Birth families may find it hard to work with social workers they consider to be instrumental in the removal of the child and may value the involvement of someone "independent".

The service works to ensure that the child is always central to the process.

Features of the service

There is no limit to the number of exchanges which can be established or the number of people who can participate. If a certain level of contact is thought to be in the best interest of a particular child then the service will accommodate it.

The arrangements (which are written down and signed, using first names only) are between the birth family, the adopters and the social worker – not between the birth family and the child. This empowers adopters and birth relatives to exchange information which may be more appropriately given to the child at a later date, or which may remain with the adoptive parents only.

In some instances, as children get older, they take over responsibility for information sent to the birth family. Responses are made from the birth family to the young person but the young person knows that their adoptive family will also receive copies.

When a birth sibling remaining in the birth family wishes to have contact independent of their family, an arrangement can often be made with another family member, such as a grandparent, who is included in the indirect contact on their behalf.

The timing of letterbox exchanges is geared towards the child's understanding. For a young child with no memory of the birth family, cards sent at birthdays or times such as Christmas may not be appropriate, but an older child may need reassurance they are remembered at such a time.

When cards are sent but contain no "information", consideration is given to ensuring that an additional exchange of information takes place at another time.

The service is for the exchange of letters, cards, photographs and materials such as children's paintings. Gifts are not considered as part of this. However, in a very small number of cases gift vouchers are included, usually for older children who might feel very confused and rejected if, for example, their grandparents stopped sending presents as before.

Once arrangements have been agreed and signed by all parties, all participants are given a copy of the document. It can be helpful for this document to be signed when the families meet during introductions. However, the service believes it is important that all negotiations and mediation are completed beforehand to avoid potential difficulties when adopters and birth relatives meet face-to-face.

In the small number of cases where no contact arrangements are established for a particular child, workers are encouraged to set up a "non-operational" letterbox. Forms are completed but not signed, reasons for the lack of indirect contact are recorded and circumstances in which it could be activated are detailed. This acts as a record in case of future requests for contact and provides the opportunity for the "door to be left open".

How it works

The social worker sends the signed arrangements and other paperwork to the Exchange. This will include names and contact details of all parties, and a little background information such as the reason the child was placed for adoption, and other details such as ethnicity, sibling relationships and whether adopters and birth parents have met.

The Co-ordinator writes to all the participants so they have a name and contact details in case they need help in the future.

A separate file is opened for the child and this eventually becomes part of their adoption file. It remains separate from the main adoption file while the information exchange continues to operate for the child. Files are retained in the child's birth name as this is the name known to all parties.

Basic information is also kept on a database. The service also keeps two index files that cross-reference the child's birth name and adopted name. This proves useful when letters are received which do not make it clear who the intended recipient is. The service says that if it was setting up the system now, it would give thought to possibly issuing participants with a reference number to quote on all correspondence. Perhaps by sending them a sheet of address labels with the individual reference number included.

When a letter is received it is opened and copied. Copies are placed on the file. All participants are clear that this will happen. Photographs and gift vouchers are copied on a scanner, in case originals are lost or destroyed.

All letters are checked for identifying information. Addresses and email addresses are removed from all letters.

The service points out that this is not simply a case of "vetting" information from birth relatives. Adoptive parents may also pass on information about children's health or behavioural problems which could cause undue anxiety to the birth family.

When the Exchange comes across information which they feel may cause distress or create problems for the recipients, the Letter Box Co-ordinator considers each case separately and considers how to respond with 'compassion, respect and flexibility'. This may involve contacting the adopters' link worker or visiting adopters and birth parents to talk through the type of information they are exchanging and helping them consider more appropriate ways of doing this.

The Exchange Service believes that: 'This kind of intervention should not be seen as too paternalistic or the local authority being unwilling to "let go". On the contrary, we have had very positive feedback from adopters and birth parents who value the responsive involvement we can provide.'

The Exchange tries to be flexible and operate one exchange where both parties prefer that the correspondence is not opened or copied. In this case the adopters believed that the birth mother would write more openly if she knew her letters were not being read first. As far as possible, the Exchange complies with this, although there are times when the outer envelope does not make it clear who the letter is for or who has sent it.

The Exchange has concluded that arrangements tend to work better when the adopters write first and the birth family replies.

Birth relatives with limited abilities are offered support with letter writing. Wherever possible, the Exchange tries to visit them to establish a relationship, and follow up is by telephone. Alternatives to letters, such as audio tapes or videos and DVDs, may also be offered to birth relatives with literacy problems. (However, the service has recently identified a number of issues around the use of videos and DVDs which it believes need very careful consideration. For example, it is difficult to monitor issues of confidentiality, videos/DVDs are likely to be "spoken" directly to the child which can make a child feel less secure in placement, children may feel uncomfortable or vulnerable about their birth family seeing a video and videos may be shown to a wide range of people. There are also issues about the durability of videos and DVDs which may be damaged or have a fairly short lifespan as technology changes.)

Where English is not the first language of the adopters or birth relatives, the Exchange will engage interpreters to support families and enable Exchange staff to understand the communication. The Exchange keeps a translation on record and also includes a translation for the child.

The form states that if any party wishes to change indirect contact arrangements they should contact the Letter Box Co-ordinator who will offer them a review. Then, every time adopters are sent information from the birth family the Exchange puts a sentence in the covering letter saying that if arrangements are not meeting the child's needs to contact the Exchange so that they can be reviewed.

The service will consider applications for changes to agreements, for example from birth relatives, but in all cases the child remains the focal point.

The service conducted a wide-ranging audit in 1999/2000 and again in 2005, to gauge perception and value of the service by all users, but also to gauge opinions from adopters and adopted young people about what they wished to happen when the young person reached 18.

(For further details of this feedback see Chapter 4, 'Through the letterbox', by Alison Vincent and Alyson Graham in *Staying Connected* (Argent, 2002).

Bibliography

A National Voice (2007) *Brothers and Sisters Survey*, London: A National Voice

Argent H (ed) (1995) *See You Soon: Contact with children looked after by local authorities*, London: BAAF

Argent H (ed) (2002) *Staying Connected: Managing contact in adoption*, London: BAAF

Argent H (2004) *What is Contact? A guide for children*, London: BAAF

Bond H (ed) (2005) *'If you don't stick with me, who will?' The challenges and rewards of foster care*, London: BAAF

Feast J (1998) *Preparing for Reunion*, London: Children's Society

Foxon J (2003) *Nutmeg Gets a Letter: Guidance notes*, London: BAAF

Macaskill C (2002) *Safe Contact: Children in permanent placement and contact with their birth relatives*, London: Russell House Publishing

Neil E and Howe D (2004) *Contact in Adoption and Permanent Foster Care: Research, theory and practice*, London: BAAF

Smith C and Logan J (2004) *After Adoption: Direct contact and relationships*, London: Routledge

Thomas C and Beckford V with Lowe N and Murch M (1999) *Adopted Children Speaking*, London: BAAF

Useful organisations

Adopt Ltd (formerly AdOPT Northern Ireland)
7 University Street
Belfast BT7 1FY
Tel: 02890 319500
Email: adoptni@aol.com

Adoption Support
Suite A, 6th Floor
Albany House
Hurst Street
Birmingham B5 4BD
Tel: 0121 666 6014
www.adoptionsupport.co.uk

Adoption UK
46 The Green, South Bar Street
Banbury OX16 9AB
Tel: 01295 752240
www.adoptionuk.org

After Adoption
12–14 Chapel Street
Salford
Manchester M3 7NH
Tel: 0161 839 4932
www.afteradoption.org.uk

After Adoption Yorkshire
31 Moor Road
Headingley
Leeds LS6 4BG
Tel: 0113 230 2100
www.afteradoptionyorkshire.org.uk

Barnardo's Scottish Adoption Advice Service
Suite 5/3, Skypark SP5
45 Finnieston Street
Glasgow G3 8JU
Tel: 0141 248 7530
www.barnardos.org.uk/saas.htm

British Association for Adoption and Fostering
Head Office
6–10 Kirby Street
London EC1N 8TS
Tel: 020 7421 2600
mail@baaf.org.uk
www.baaf.org.uk

BAAF Scotland
40 Shandwick Place
Edinburgh EH2 4RT
Tel: 0131 220 4749

BAAF Cymru
7 Cleeve House
Lambourne Crescent
Cardiff CF14 5GP
Tel: 029 2074 7934

BAAF Northern Ireland
Botanic House
1–5 Botanic Avenue
Belfast BT7 1JG

Fostering Network
87 Blackfriars Road
London SE1 8HA
Tel: 020 7620 6400
www.fostering.net

Fostering Network Scotland
Ingram House, 2nd Floor
Glasgow G1 1DA
Tel: 0141 204 1400

Fostering Network Wales
Suite 11, 2nd Floor
Bay Chambers
West Bute Street
Cardiff Bay CF10 5BB
Tel: 029 2044 0940

Post Adoption Centre
5 Torriano Mews
Torriano Avenue
London NW5 2RZ
Tel: 020 7284 0555
www.postadoptioncentre.org.uk

Other titles on contact

Contact in Adoption and Permanent Foster Care: Research, theory and practice
Edited by Elsbeth Neil and David Howe

This book gathers together the latest thoughts and research findings of many of the leading authorities on the subject of contact in adoption and permanent foster care.

An essential reference work...this one encourages careful thinking about plans for children in permanent care, taking into account the relevant issues of the planning process.

Community Care
ISBN 1 903699 60 6
2004

Staying Connected: Managing contact in adoption
Edited by Hedi Argent

An anthology which examines and describes the making, sustaining and evaluating of contact arrangements. Contributors offer varied practice examples to explore what works and what does not, and why.

ISBN 1 903699 12 6
2002

What is Contact? A guide for children
Hedi Argent

This booklet describes what contact or "keeping in touch" means for children who are not living with their birth families. It discusses the many ways in which contact with family and friends can be maintained, and includes case studies that illustrate contact in a range of settings.

ISBN 1 903699 59 2
2004

Contact: Managing visits to children
Peg McCartt Hess and Kathleen Ohman Proch

A handbook containing valuable guidance on good practice in arranging and managing visits.

ISBN 1 873868 12 X
1993

All the above are available from BAAF Publications.
Tel: 020 7421 2604
Saffron House
6–10 Kirby Street
London EC1N 8TS
www.baaf.org.uk

Registered charity 275689

www.baaf.org.uk